Unheard Voices

D0544650

Unheard Voices

JEFFREY HESKINS

DARTON·LONGMAN + TODD

First published in 2001 by
Darton, Longman and Todd Ltd
1 Spencer Court
140–142 Wandsworth High Street
London SW18 4JJ

ISBN 0–232–52427–0

A catalogue record for this book is available from the British Library.

Designed by Sandie Boccacci
Phototypeset in 9.5/13.25pt Palatino by Intype London Ltd
Printed and bound in Great Britain by
The Bath Press, Bath

CONTENTS

FOREWORD

by Richard Holloway

Most people are familiar with the phenomenon of unconscious trauma, leading to the referred pain of phobia and anxiety. Some event deep in the past, buried beneath memory, still works upon us, causing psychic pain and paralysing fear. Repressed memories are a frequent source of human pain; but so are those parts of ourselves we cannot own, such as unadmitted sexual longings, which take their revenge by projecting themselves onto others upon whom we can discharge our own self-loathing. This was a pattern Nietzsche understood long before Freud:

> Every sufferer instinctively seeks a cause for his suffering; more exactly, an agent; still more specifically, a guilty agent who is susceptible to suffering – in short, some living thing upon which he can, on some pretext or other, vent his affects, actually or in effigy: for the venting of his affects represents the greatest attempt on the part of the suffering to win relief, *anaesthesia*, the narcotic he cannot help desiring to deaden pain of any kind.[1]

There is an ugly example of this in the film *American Beauty* in the person of the tough, manly, fascist American marine captain who lives next door to the Kevin Spacey character. It is obvious that the tightly-coiled soldier is a deeply conflicted person, whose self-hatred shows itself in violence towards his son and contempt of anything approaching liberal values. His son is supplying the Spacey character with the happy weed marijuana, but the captain thinks their relationship is sexual. Persuaded that Spacey is gay, he makes a pass at him and is gently rebuffed. Unable to live with the truth that has just been revealed, he kills the man he has just tried to make love to. He kills in his neighbour what he cannot live with in his own nature. Homophobia is not the only example of this phenomenon, but it is an extremely powerful one, particularly in religious institutions, and it is rife in the Anglican Church.

The Lambeth Conference of 1998 will be remembered as a particularly ugly example of collective homophobia. One Church of England bishop likened it to a Nuremberg rally, and the comparison was apt. Those of us who lived through that infamous afternoon of debate on human sexuality are unlikely to have witnessed such hatred and cruel contempt anywhere else. In my own case, it produced in me an allergic distaste for episcopal gatherings, and I still battle to control feelings of contempt for otherwise liberal-minded bishops who made little attempt to contest what was happening. As far as the English bishops were concerned, I suspect that the motive behind their complicity in the event was institutional prudence rather than moral passion. In moments like this, the logic of Caiaphas prevails: it is always expedient to sacrifice the innocent for the sake of the institution. The deepest irony in all of this is that it is all done in the name of the man of Nazareth whose most cutting anger was reserved for leaders who sacrifice individuals for the sake of the institutions they serve. Rather than this sort of managerial cowardice, he offered prophetic challenge to the powers that be, no matter the cost.

Prophetic action operates on two levels at once: it challenges us to look to God's future and it invites us to live as though it were already here. In other words, it puts justice ahead of our own comfort and calls us to create communities where God's justice and mercy are already in operation. When the Anglican Church agonised over the ordination of women one of the main arguments against it was that it would divide the Church, so it was expedient to sacrifice justice for the sake of institutional unity. Fortunately, that voice did not prevail; and it was argued that ordaining women was a prophetic act that foreshadowed God's righteousness. The same dynamic is being repeated in the campaign for justice for gay and lesbian people in the Church. In that campaign *Unheard Voices* can be interpreted as a prophetic tract for our times. Like all prophecy, *Unheard Voices* operates on two levels. On the immediate level, it introduces us to a prophetic community in the parish church of St Luke's, Charlton. For 20 years this parish has offered services of blessing for gay and lesbian couples living in the local community. Said like that, it sounds unremarkable; given the climate of opinion in the Church of England and the attitude of its bishops, it is a profoundly radical stance to have adopted. This group of people has simply chosen to act as though God's justice and love were already the official policy of its ecclesiastical superiors. These changes always assume a momentousness they do not deserve, as though the heavens would fall when we make marginal adjustments to the ways we organise our human communities. One of the beauties of this book is that it shows the ordinariness of the matter, the undramatic but deeply honest struggles of people struggling to be faithful to their love for one another. 'This is what it feels like', the book tells us, 'so why not try it for yourselves.'

But the book operates on another level: it is something of a primer for churches that want to rise to the same challenge, but are not sure how to go about it. *Unheard Voices* helps us to understand the theological and psychological issues behind the homosexuality debate, but it also offers practical advice on the creation of appropriate liturgies for same-sex blessings, as well as models of preparation for those who are committing themselves in love to the promised state. And all of this comes in a book that is unremarkably unpolemical, in spite of the contentious nature of its topic. That, too, may be prophetic: in 20 years' time we'll probably all wonder what the fuss was about.

CHAPTER 1

In Search of the Unheard Voices

from gossip to gospel

For more than 20 years St Luke's, Charlton has been blessing same-sex unions. 'The church that marries the gays' first attracted press attention in 1979. Since then the debate about sex and gender nationally has often become repetitive. Yet there are voices that are seldom, if ever, heard in the adversarial proceedings of synod and council. At local level they call for Gospel values, consensus and the truth – and they are heard poignantly in the story which follows, as a particular Christian community in south-east London tells it.

The story begins for me in 1988 when I became a vicar in the Kidbrooke Team Ministry. Kidbrooke and Charlton are neighbouring parishes divided by a busy trunk road and this has the effect of preventing any real interaction between the two church communities. However, rumour and gossip are no respecters of parish boundaries, and stories of St Luke's sometimes filtered across the main road to St Nicholas, Kidbrooke where I was based. Some members of my new parish community described St Luke's as progressive in its outlook, but for others, its stand on issues such as the ordination of women and its pastoral care of lesbian and gay people were sometimes seen as 'way out' and eccentric. Levels of prejudice in the wider community meant that, as vicar of St Nicholas, I had occasional requests to baptise Charlton babies because the parents did not like St Luke's 'gay connection'.

Seven years later, this received 'rumour and gossip' from one side of the road did not match my experience on the other. In 1995

I moved to the parish of Charlton and as rector of St Luke's the same story appeared in an entirely different light as I began to get to know my new congregation – and to encounter those same-sex couples who were looking for God's blessing on their unions.

I had expected to find more evidence of a 'specialised' and high-profile ministry of support for lesbian and gay couples, but nothing could have been further from the truth. There were no policy documents or pastoral guidelines, nor any kind of record showing what levels and kind of support was offered to same-gender couples. In many respects St Luke's reveals itself as a fairly traditional catholic Anglican church, particularly in its style of worship. There is the general round of weddings and christenings and funerals. It seems to be an ancient parish church in an ordinary urban setting with little to suggest that it is either odd or extreme.

My study at the rectory looks out on the ancient churchyard at the back of St Luke's – now a memorial garden. It is an important place for many people in the local community. For some it is the only time that they venture near the church and I am often moved when I see the devotion of so many to the memory of those that they have loved in life and who have now died. Whatever else cemeteries and memorial gardens are, they are certainly places in which stories are to be found. The stories can be seen in the names and epitaphs on gravestones and memorial markers. Some tell of family affection: 'In our hearts you will always stay.' Others hold to the hope of reunion: 'Together at last, Gertrude and Sidney.' The memorials of children speak from the hearts of parents longing for the assurance that, beyond death, their much-loved child is in a place of safety. One reads 'Safe in the arms of Jesus', and another 'Now in the arms of his Grandad'. Between a memorial for Daisy, aged 64, and that for Michael and Gwen, who both lived into their eighties, is the one for Rodney Madden who died in 1995. His epitaph reads 'I'll see you in the morning, darling.' They might have been words spoken by Michael to Gwen, or Gertrude to Sidney – but Rodney was gay, and they were spoken by Saxon, his partner of 35 years, every night as they put the light out before sleep.

Saxon's cremated remains were recently buried alongside Rod's in accordance with his funeral wishes. The mourners seemed much like any other group coming to make their farewells: flowers were laid and words of affection publicly pronounced. The scene was unremarkable, but behind it lay a remarkable story. Rodney and Saxon were an openly gay couple and were committed Christians; that was the obvious part of the story. But they had come to live out that openness within a church community that was prepared to support them and live openly alongside them. Some of the story had been documented in journalistic fashion by the press, but much of it remained in the experience of older members of the congregation. It had been passed on, as stories often are, with varying degrees of dilution or exaggeration.

More tangible than the epitaphs in the churchyard are the voices of those people who sit in the pews at St Luke's Sunday by Sunday. Rodney and Saxon's story is an important part of their history. Part of the purpose of this book will be to retrieve and tell that story. Some, like James who can remember will give their own first-hand accounts of the events and the controversy.

> When the occasion came that they had requested their union to be blessed in church, to which the rector had agreed, Saxon's mother came to it. She said that she wasn't entirely in favour of it, but she felt that she had to support her son. We sat with her in the front of the church.   *(James)*

Others, like Sara who has joined St Luke's in recent years, will describe how they came to hear the story and the impact it has had upon them.

> I got to hear about it because there was something in the parish bulletin. That's the only time I was thinking about it. I don't have an opinion one way or another. I thought, O well! That's just a reflection of this community's diversity again.   *(Sara)*

Teenage members of the church will share their views on a story that they have grown up with and which has, in part, helped to form their life in the Christian community and influence their view of the wider Church.

> Just because church leaders don't agree with blessing the couples doesn't mean that it is not right. *(Eddy)*

> We should definitely do it. It raises awareness and we don't want any of this brushing under the carpet. *(Alex)*

Within two weeks of being licensed to the parish I received a request for a service of blessing and covenanted union from Amelia and Ruth. Having no idea as to how I might begin and remain consistent with the ethos that I had inherited in this new parish, I proceeded to meet them and find out what exactly they were wanting. Amelia and Ruth were by no means the first same-gender couple that I had met nor was it my first experience of a service of union and blessing for such a couple. Like numerous clergy I had been involved in similar pastoral liturgies previously, but always quietly, if not secretly, and usually with members of a congregation, which meant that they were people who were known to me. Amelia and Ruth proved to be a couple who had given extensive thought to why it was important to make vows in church. In the absence of any formal guidelines or any pastoral liturgy at the church we were left to make our own way in preparing a service that would be meaningful and sincere. Amelia and Ruth attended the Sunday Eucharist on several occasions and took time to meet those members of the congregation who would be 'staffing' the church on the occasion of their service of blessing. We met four times to discuss the content of the service and its tone. They enjoyed a fine day and a ceremony that was thoughtful and moving.

> The service of blessing gave meaning to our feelings for one another . . . it was serious and was taken seriously. *(Amelia)*

Amelia and Ruth were the first couple in my time to test the St Luke's 'parish policy' initiated by the service of blessing for Saxon and Rodney. Since then I have met 15 other couples asking for similar ministry, of whom 12 have continued with preparation and proceeded to a covenant service. Over the last 21 years 45 couples have sought and received a service of blessing. The numbers may not be enormous, but the voices of those couples who have persisted – often over a number of years – in a quest to make vows to each other publicly must, I believe, be heard by the wider Church.

A week after Ruth and Amelia's service I met a clergy colleague at the crematorium. He asked me how I was getting along in the new parish and then, after looking furtively over both shoulders as if about to impart some top-secret information, whispered from behind his hand, 'Have you done any gay marriages yet?' As one now on the 'inside', I found this kind of conversation increasingly odd and silly. My view of a ministry to same-gender couples as well as to this new church and parish was already changing.

The story which lies behind Rodney and Saxon's small plot in the memorial garden goes back to 1978 when they came to St Luke's – the first openly gay couple to take a full share in the life of the church community. They had already been together nearly 20 years and after they read an article by the then rector, Tony Crowe, they approached him to see if they could have their union blessed in church. His acceptance of them, and their subsequent acceptance by the church community, encouraged the couple to sell their house and move to Charlton.

Their service of blessing took place in 1979. There was a small congregation and the service drew some adverse press coverage. Stories circulate that the 39 Articles of Religion from the Church of England *Book of Common Prayer* were nailed to the church door.

Six years later in 1985, to mark their twenty-fifth anniversary, a Eucharist of thanksgiving was celebrated in St Luke's. Rodney and Saxon took part as altar servers. The clergy led the service, the choir sang and the youth group provided musical accompaniment. A private video recorded at the time reveals it to have been a very ordinary and quite 'traditional' service attended by about 100 members of the congregation and friends. Again it was the subject of some protest. There was picketing outside the church and the rector later suffered physical attack and had his car vandalised. The video shows the pulpit being 'occupied' by an uninvited young man posing as an itinerant preacher. Waving his Bible he began an extemporised sermon:

> Beloved, now you must listen to the Word of God. God is proclaiming his truth today and is proclaiming his truth because he loves you, and loves you dearly. I come because I love Saxon and Rodney. God loves you but God cannot bless this meeting. God cannot bless homosexuality because God is righteous and God is love. This is the Word of God the Bible so readily proclaims to us.

He then quoted extensively from St Paul's letter to the Romans before being escorted to the door shouting:

> O that we might repent of this terrible sin. God loves you; Jesus Christ loves you; but you must know the truth.

There is little doubt that the ceremony and the feelings evoked by it marked a watershed in the life of the congregation. Some were deeply wounded by the intrusion into what was perceived as a family gathering. Others were angry at the open way in which the event became public knowledge. The reporting of these events in parts of the national press was largely sensationalist and trite, bearing little resemblance to the events as captured on film and in the memories of those who were there.

Not a Gay Day for Rodney

A church service to celebrate the twenty-five year 'marriage' of two gay lovers ended in uproar yesterday . . . Angry parishioners invaded the pulpit . . . another parishioner urged God 'not to destroy the church'.[1]

Pulpit stormed as gay couple celebrate their 'silver wedding'

A Church of England service to celebrate a homosexual

couple's 25-year 'marriage' was interrupted by protesters who denounced it as evil. One barged past the white-robed, middle-aged men, stormed the pulpit and delivered an impromptu sermon condemning homosexuality as a sin and the ceremony as 'wicked' and 'depraved' . . .[2]

Rumpus as gay couple are blessed

. . . Homosexuals Saxon Lucas and Rodney Madden dressed in white for the service to celebrate 25 years of 'togetherness'. But just as the ceremony began, two protesters barged into the pulpit . . . Rodney, a 46-year-old actor burst into tears and theatrical designer Saxon 52, sat stunned. The demonstrators, who described themselves as 'Warriors of God' were escorted from St Luke's church in Charlton, South London.[3]

For others there was the confusion of reconciling the feelings that they had for two men who had become well-liked in the local congregation and their desire to espouse the values of faithfulness and openness, with the reaction of some Christian and other neighbouring groups. For some, there was an irony in the proclamation by the uninvited preacher that contrasted with the message given in a vote of thanks at the end of the service. While both were messages of 'love', the meanness of spirit with which the first was delivered merely heightened the generosity of the second.

I would like to extend my own grateful thanks to the parish of St Luke's for the support and love we have been given since we came here. I don't think that two people, irrespective of their sexuality could have had as much support and love as we receive in this parish. It is a wonderful parish full of wonderful, caring, people and I thank you all for the great happiness we have had here. (*Saxon*)

When Rodney Madden and Saxon Lucas arrived at St Luke's Charlton in 1979 they broke important ground for the congregation. They challenged the Christian community to take their partnership seriously. Since then others have arrived, not always wanting to

7

join the church membership, but posing the same challenge. Will the Christian community take them seriously? Nobody seems to have left the church on account of either the first service of blessing for an openly gay couple or for the celebration of their 'silver jubilee'. On the contrary it had the effect of addressing that challenge. Was it really possible publicly to welcome and support a gay or lesbian couple? How could they use this experience to serve the wider parish neighbourhood? What should they do about people who perceived themselves as excluded from the community life of the Church or confined to its margins? Was it possible to go on with this kind of care when it seemed so remote from the interests of the wider Church and was now officially disapproved of by the bishops?

The immediate effect of this experience brought about a commitment to talk with each other as a congregation and with neighbouring congregations holding different views. The result of these discussions led to a new phase of pastoral action. The Parochial Church Council made a decision to serve those gay and lesbian couples who came seeking the support of the local parish church with a ministry of blessing and affirmation of the partnerships. It would be a ministry that would continue at the discretion of the parish clergy.

Saxon and Rodney remained at St Luke's for several years where they took a full part in the life of the church. They lived openly and happily within that community before moving away to live in the West Country. They remained in touch with many of their former friends from St Luke's, but it seems as though they never found another church offering the same degree of support. Evidence for this was found on the night that Saxon brought Rodney 'home' to St Luke's. For many the story that accompanied it was justification alone for the need to continue an open support for gay and lesbian couples. In 1995 Rodney died and Saxon brought his cremated remains to St Luke's for burial. For him, and others who witnessed it, the funeral service had been a disaster. Saxon had been virtually ignored and was mentioned nowhere in the presiding minister's funeral address. There was no acknowledgement of him as Rodney's life partner, nor his part in nursing him through serious illness until death. Instead the minister lamented the absence of Rodney's 'real' family who had been unable to leave their home in Australia to travel to the funeral in England.

Stories of this kind of 'enforced anonymity' are all too common in accounts of bereavement amongst same-gender couples. With no legal status to their unions, the surviving partner in such a relationship is often overlooked as next of kin, unable to take a prominent part in the funeral arrangements. Unless there is a sympathetic minister or a church community to support such a couple, it is likely that the insensitivity revealed in Saxon's experience will be repeated. Government legislation would go a long way to assisting those gay and lesbian couples for whom legal standing is important. Secure relationships are surely a freedom that all citizens should be able to enjoy. Is the wish to live openly, visibly and safely in community life supported by a legal infrastructure such an unreasonable request? These are questions that have emerged for our church community in Charlton. They have arisen because of a specific experience that has changed us and the way we think about relationships. But they are questions that all Christians might wrestle with, and what follows is an illustration of how one community set about addressing them. It begins with a commitment to the kind of listening that has been absent from so much of the ongoing debate on gay and lesbian relationships and our life together in the Christian community.

Listening to the story

This book has a definite story to tell. In telling it the church members reveal their commitment to listening to the voices of that story. Though voices of the past, they have influenced the shape of the community in the present. Rodney's death in 1995 marked an important ending for much of the church community at St Luke's. They began to realise that Rodney and Saxon's relationship, while they had been members of St Luke's, had influenced and changed their thinking and their lives as a Christian community.

The effect of this experience was quite powerful and was summarised in a Church Council meeting early in 1996.

> I have sometimes had the feeling that one or two 'enlightened' people have in the past tried to rush things through before people were ready to go with it. If you take the women's issue thing. We became more open to the women's issue by having women ministers around who wanted to be priests. We learned by having the experience and then when we had the experience of Rodney and Saxon in the congregation, it helped us learn. I think that Rodney and Saxon were a catalyst in this situation. *(George)*

What George seems to be saying is that the church community was able to learn and grow when it *listened* to its experience. He cites the ordination of women as a different example. Sharing the experience of women who wanted to be ordained, but at the time could not be, enabled significant change in attitude and thinking within St Luke's congregation. Action without reflection is not a good way of living as community. What he goes on to suggest is that a discussion in the abstract will be less significant for this particular congregation than one that begins with something they really know about and with which they can identify. The experience of an openly gay couple in the congregation had made a difference to the church community, but it was rapidly becoming history. There was now a need to see what difference it had made to them as a congregation with almost 20 years' hindsight. In doing this, the story and its influence would not simply die with the couple.

As we began the process of recovery in 1996, the Parochial Church Council (PCC) agreed to a congregational day workshop discussing issues around human sexuality. It was a first step on the way to recovering this important story in the life of the church. It would influence attitudes towards and pastoral care of not only gay and lesbian couples, but also other categories of people who felt discriminated against both in and outside the Church. In 1998 the PCC sanctioned a collection of memories, reflections and views from within the congregation and amongst gay and lesbian couples. These were obtained through tape-recorded interviews. The results form the basis of this book.

Listening to the context

There is also a commitment to listening to context in this book. Life in the local church cannot be formed and sustained in a vacuum. While I am interested in recovering a local story and hearing some new voices speak from their experiences, it is also important that this story bears some reference to the wider discussion that is going on in the Church and elsewhere. Chapters Two and Three give attention to this. I have been struck by the similarities between attitudes and responses to gay and lesbian relationships in the Church and in other parts of public life. That this is a necessarily 'theoretical' chapter leaves the way open for the new 'voices' of local church community and gay and lesbian couples to speak from experience. The reader will see these emerge in their own right later in the book.

Listening to the language

Listening to new voices has meant paying attention to how we use religious language. Church worship often seems to be very 'wordy'. I find increasingly depressing the way that so much language used by the Church manages to alienate so many of the people it is called to serve. What the exercise in listening has done is to show how ordinary Christians can talk about God and Church in language that makes sense in their everyday lives. During the interviews with couples I was constantly struck by the way many described the spiritual significance of what they were doing. There was no attempt to borrow specialist language to describe what, if anything, they understood of God. Most were able to do this in simple and un-fussy terms. Steve discovers God in an unexpected and refreshing image.

This ceremony has made me think about life and other
people and how important other people are. There are lots
of different people in life and so it is important not to make
assumptions. One thing that impressed me when we came
and had a look around St Luke's and all the people were
there; they were just ordinary everyday people who are
perfectly happy to take other people at face value. There
was a great feeling of togetherness and I think that God is
togetherness amongst people. I probably didn't realise that
before.

Steve has no use for complicated ecclesial expressions. He has
already discovered a language with which to describe his search
for meaning and purpose. Time and again the interviews turned
up evidence that ordinary people, from all walks of life, are quite
capable of sharing in the work of theology, but rarely get the
chance. Most would never consider it to be their business. Indeed,
some of those participating in this research, when asked about
God, described themselves as ill qualified to think like that. This
example, and others which will appear later, are an encouragement
to get the people in our congregations and local communities to
participate in the theological reflection of the Church. It is a sad
state of affairs if the only insights can be gleaned in the Church
from the 'top, down'. By retreating to the classroom to do the work
of theology, we disengage from insights like these. In listening to
their experience of meeting each other, both church members and
couples find positive images of God as hospitality, sanctuary
and empowerment. Like Steve they first discover these images in
each other. They find welcome, safety and a place of meeting that
releases them from a prejudiced way of thinking about each other.

   The reader will see that the self-perceptions of the church
members are often confirmed by what gay and lesbian couples
experience when they meet them. Moira, on the one hand, can
describe the way she sees her church community in open and
generous terms.

It has a fairly liberal, tolerant attitude, supporting people in different walks of life and trying to make everybody feel part of the community.

Steve, on the other hand, can verify that perception whilst describing his feelings on first meeting 'the church'.

> I think that we were both nervous the first time we met the clergy, but we soon felt at ease. They were just very easy to be with and treated us as if we were ordinary regular people.

Thus the Church lives and grows – in the real world – by meeting people and challenging previously unchallenged perceptions. The commitment to listening must lead to a second commitment of self-examination. New insight produces altered perception. Some of the couples that approached the church were surprised that it was so open to them. This contrasted with their perceived view of the Church via the media. Church members found their perceptions of 'gay' and 'lesbian' challenged at a quite basic level. One of the couples included a partner who was a senior citizen. A church member remarked that they had always, for no logical reason, thought of gay and lesbian people as young. Another of the couples had a partner who was disabled and attended the service of covenanted union in a wheelchair. From these experiences came new perceptions of each other. Couples and church members came to alter the way they thought about each other.

Couples wanting services of blessing often arrived with high levels of anxiety and a fear of rejection. Chapter Four listens to these anxieties and asks, what is it that brings people to seek out the ministry of the Church in such a climate? Often low levels of self-worth accompany this insecurity, feelings which have only been healed thanks to the faithful commitment and care of their partner. The couple's expectations of the Church are low. One couple thought it would be a matter of going to the church on their own with the priest 'when nobody was around,' and being blessed quietly in a side chapel. I often wonder why gay and lesbian couples bother with the Church at all when it would seem that so much of it has contributed to their sense of rejection and unwantedness.

The counter side of rejection and ridicule is found in the themes of acceptance and the underlying desire to be taken seriously by the Church. This is also pursued in Chapter Four. The couples speak movingly of their longing to be accepted and seen as a serious relationship. What is interesting is the seriousness with which they themselves view the Church and what it has to offer. It is a far cry from the popular image of the irrelevant institution in an advanced state of decay. For several couples, the Church wears the mantle of divine authority. To be accepted by the Church was to have God's acceptance pronounced. This is a powerful perception. Chris and Paul risk repetition of the rejection they experienced in one church because they see the Church as God's agency. For them finding a church is important because the search for acceptance and the desire to be taken seriously is so strong.

> For me it was that we were being accepted by the Church and that we were being accepted by God. This was particularly important to me because of the experience I'd had in a previous church where I was basically shunned if I led a gay lifestyle. *(Chris)*

All couples undergo a period equivalent to marriage preparation. This time is spent in order to ease some of these anxieties. It also affords time to reflect on what each couple is *really* asking for when they make an approach. Much is made of whether such services for gay and lesbian couples can be classified as marriage and it is sometimes claimed, by Christians who disapprove, that this kind of support for lesbian and gay couples undermines marriage. Such a view seems to suggest a lack of sincerity on the part of the couples, perhaps implying that they are not serious about commitment in relationship. I have to say that this has not been my experience of the couples I have worked with. Most do not want to copy a heterosexual marriage service when they make their vows, but they struggle to translate their desire for commitment and faithfulness into a language that they see as belonging to the Church. Thus they are forced to use the language of marriage to describe what they want, simply because there is no other sacred language to use. I can see no hard evidence at all to support the claim that gay and lesbian couples wanting to make faithful vows to each other are somehow undermining hetero-sexual couples wanting to do the same. Rather the contrary is true, and while we are careful at St Luke's explicitly to use the language of 'blessing' rather than 'marriage', there are some couples who would like to be married and some who, if reticent about marriage at the beginning of their preparation, wish for the framework of marriage by the end.

> Previously I was not comfortable with the term marriage and Paul wanted that . . . I had wanted to call it a service of commitment.
>
> It is a marriage as far as our friends and family are concerned and as far as we feel. So, yes, I consider myself married, but if they legalised marriage for us tomorrow I would do the service again so that it could be legal.   *(Chris)*

Chapters Five and Six find church members and couples wrest-ling with the language of blessing, marriage and what it means to make a Christian response to gay and lesbian couples seeking the support of the Church.

Some couples bring stories of rejection that are quite painful to hear. Others describe their own ordinary families wrestling with the idea that a son or daughter, or brother or sister, or mum or dad might be gay or lesbian. Some bring wonderful stories of acceptance or reconciliation. The themes of hospitality, sanctuary and empowerment emerge in Chapter Seven, challenging the Church to become a community of true inclusion. A new com-munity of inclusion would go a long way to healing the wounds of rejection and alienation. I have long been interested in the revival of the Church's healing ministry. However, in recent years I have come to see that ministry as lacking a social and political dimension. By that I mean that we have become so individualistic in our Western European and North American culture that we are rapidly losing our sense of belonging to each other. Infamous statements such as the often reported 'There is no such thing as society – there are only individuals,'[4] are a sign of that trend. I think that there are clear signs in the gospel narratives that point to the healing ministry of Jesus as more than a mere preoccupation with the personal health of a sequence of individuals. There is a sense in which that ministry becomes the focus for the reconciliation of fragmented communities and I think that there is good evidence in the New Testament to suggest that the earliest Christian communities might have seen it that way too. Thus, in this book I am not very interested in the claims of some Christians for the 'healing' of homosexual orientation in selected individuals. Instead, I am keen to pursue what I see as the Gospel concept of community healing through reconciliation, and that unless *all* are healed/reconciled, then *none* are.

The reader will see that my use of Scripture is interpretative and has been confined, by and large, to this single chapter on healing and reconciliation. I have made no attempt to address the usual texts drawn on to discuss the issue of same-sex attraction. These have been well attended to by others who have produced work with varying conclusions. Some of these books will be listed in the Select Bibliography.

I am aware that much has already been written on the subject of gay and lesbian relationships. There is a wealth of good material in areas of biblical scholarship and sexual ethics from diverse and often diametrically opposed views. Many of those contributions have been offered through approaches using the social sciences and psychoanalysis. There have been historical analyses and examination of sociological change. Of particular significance has been the emergence of numerous gay and lesbian writers who have shared an experience and offered new theological perspectives born of those experiences. For some it will seem strange to write yet more on what seems already to be an oversubscribed subject.

Having outlined some of the main themes of the book, I have

to confess that what it contains is partly born of a sense of frustration with an ongoing discussion in the Church and elsewhere that has revealed its participants as seemingly incapable of living with differences and disagreement. However, the reason for writing is not only driven by the desire to jump off the maddening roundabout of name-calling, platitudes and defensively erected polarised positions. What makes this contribution to the ongoing discussion different is that it is a local, grass roots contribution. It chronicles the views of a diverse parish church community – views they themselves have gleaned. The method for doing this is not unique and readers familiar with some aspects of liberation theology will see that for themselves. Essentially this is a book which records everyday Christian people thinking about what they are doing in pastoral action and how they are able to draw images of God from it. This is practical theology done in a practical way.

It is different because, although the church community drew some very clear conclusions from the exercise, you, the reader, are left to make up your own mind on the matter. I am not committed to 'winning the argument' in this book. Attempts to have the final word, and legislate for all, have done little more than scar the debate on same-sex love and relationships within the Church.

It is also different because I think that it provides an example of how churches need to tell the stories of their communities. Wherever people have gathered in the history of the human race, stories have been told. In countless cultures, tribes and families, the stories of their formation and continuation are a key factor. Any community living in the present and looking to the future is shaped by the past. Church communities are no different and what you will find here is a commitment to recovering a story that has made an impact on local church life at a deep level. But I hope that it will also be clear that the recovery of and telling of stories like this can change communities of people and the ways in which churches go about their business of serving the neighbourhood in which they are located. The voices of the gay and lesbian couples who have been to St Luke's seem to bear out this view.

Finally, I think that this book is different because it is about difference and how being different can be a positive thing. So many within the Church are unable to live with this understanding of life in community. In our parish community, we try to have open disagreement and still remain an integrated and vibrant community ready to serve God in the wider world. For a discussion that has been dogged by hostility, misunderstanding and calls for punitive action in the wider Church, this book is written as a positive contribution to an ongoing search for understanding.

> Our sexual affections can no more define who we are than can our class, race or nationality. At the deepest ontological level, therefore, there is no such thing as 'a' homosexual or 'a' heterosexual; there are human beings, male and female, called to redeemed humanity in Christ, endowed with a complex variety of emotional potentialities and threatened by a complex variety of forms of alienation.[5]

Michael Doe concludes his book on the Church and homosexuality with this quote from the report of the sub-section on human sexuality at the Lambeth Conference 1998. At one level I have much sympathy for its sentiments. To be defined solely by sexual orientation is pitiful. We are called to a full humanity and so I too, like many of the contributors here, am surprised at the way discussion in the Church on gay and lesbian relationships still produces more heat than light. In 1979 one experience in our local church brought us into contact with human beings in need. This experience faced us with questions of inclusiveness. Who is 'in' and who is 'out' within the life of a church congregation? Who is within the remit of the parish community and who is outside it? The distinctions of sexual orientation have become, for us, insignificant. Instead of defining people by sexual orientation it becomes instead just a part of the way we describe each other.

Researching and putting this book together has involved many people and taken much of their time and energy. It has been important to produce it in this way for two reasons. Firstly, that it might not be dismissed as no more than the work of a single 'maverick mouthpiece' and secondly, genuinely to allow new voices the freedom to enter the discussion. The Church is not of a common mind on the matter of gay and lesbian partnerships and I am aware that what is here will most likely evoke a variety of responses from the scandalised to the relieved. Whatever the response of the individual reader I hope that it will be received as a contribution to what is an ongoing discussion and an ongoing process of learning what it means to live and work as Christians in community.

CHAPTER 2

The Same Old Voices?

the context

> Theology that is contextual realises that culture, history,
> contemporary thought forms, and so forth, are to be
> considered, along with scripture and tradition, as valid
> forms for theological expression.[1]

Why appeal to context at all?

Christianity is a religion founded on the life of Jesus, a particular
individual living in a particular time and place. Because of this the
Church has always had to engage itself in the struggle to interpret
its central message in changing times and places. Most of the
material collected for this book has enabled it to focus on a specific
local context and a particular time frame. That material has been
collected within and by members of the Anglican Church community in Charlton, London, and by six lesbian and gay couples
who had prepared for and participated in services of covenanted
union to bless their partnerships. If the context of where and how
we live makes any difference to how we think about God and each
other, then we have to pay some attention to the present human
experience. This book is an attempt to record that experience and
its affect upon one community.

It has been guided by a commitment to the idea that the same
issue may be viewed differently in different times and places.
Everything we try to understand is affected by our context. The
work of theology has usually been seen as the attempt to explore
and discover God's presence in the world. The work of contextual
theology commits us to the idea that although the love of God is

constant it may be expressed in different ways, according to context. God is thus revealed in new ways in different situations. What this book is attempting to provide is a faithful record of a local church community paying attention to the influences of local context in its formation of good pastoral practices. Those practices will affect everyone that the local church meets in the expression of its ministry, but will take particular account of gay and lesbian couples. So, while this is a book focusing specifically on gay and lesbian couples, much of what it has to say could be applied consistently to any who visit or join the church, or who come asking for its help.

What needs to be recognised is that to make reference to this local context in isolation from other contextual influences would deny the degree of change that is brought about for individuals and local communities by wider social influences. The attitude of church members from any community engaged in a reflective exercise on how it welcomes same-gender couples will be formed largely by their experiences as a community and as individuals. However, they will also be shaped by the continuing story of the human race and how, in different cultures and in different ages, that story has changed. The appeal to context is one that takes seriously that change and what the sources of influence have been.

In one sense we can see that this is not a new appeal. Various writers in the field of Contextual Theology[2] are able to trace its source to what are often described as the 'liberation countries'. Traditional Theology, by which I mean theological thinking and writing that is rooted in Europe and North America, has often claimed that contextual theology is something of a false dichotomy. This group of writers will say that they have always tried to relate the data of 'tradition' to reality. While that may be a laudable thing, it is not the same as contextual theology. Relating what has been the received mode of theological thinking falls more into the realms of what is often called Applied Theology. It is a scholarly and academic form of theology that allows the ideas of the scholarly world to be applied to the culture contexts of the real world. Contextual theology tries to work differently.

Rather than trying, in the first instance, to apply a received theology to a local context, this new kind of theology began with an examination of the context itself. In contexts where issues of conflict and oppression were paramount, a lengthy analysis of relationships of power and injustice was clearly called for. Social, economic and political questions engaged the energies that had once been devoted to philosophical or metaphysical questions.[3]

So contextual theology seems to have a different starting place. It places great emphasis and value upon our own experience. Doing it this way, we try to turn theology on its head. Unlike the so called 'traditional' theology of the universities and seminaries, which seems to keep theology as the preserve of the scholarly academic, I am trying to value the insights of everyday life lived as much by the postman as the professor. Contextual theology is a way of thinking about God in the local situation. More than this, it specifically values everyday lives as the best supply of experience. This book wants to give voices to the owners of such experiences and reinstate their contributions as valid theological reflection while also recognising the value of the trained theology teacher/minister.

What becomes clear as the context is taken seriously in theology, is that theology can never be understood as a finished product produced by experts, which is merely delivered into a Christian community for its consumption. On the other hand, theology cannot be the mere recording of what people think. Theology must be an activity of dialogue emerging out of mutual respect between faithful, but not technically trained people and faithful and listening professionals.[4]

This way of doing theology has been most widely appreciated in church communities belonging to Third World continents, but where it has successfully travelled into European and North American thinking contextual theology has allowed for the restoration of the social and political dimension to theology generally. This has allowed it to give particular freshness to biblical analysis. Entire communities have been able to approach the Scriptures in a new way. This in turn has given birth to the more politically driven Liberation theologies of Africa and Latin America. Communities experiencing the effects of social, political and economic alienation have been able to effectively protest through their church communities by being able to see themselves in the Scriptures as the poor and marginalised for whom God has particular care. This has radically altered their understanding of what it means to live together in community and what it means to be 'Church'.

It might be nearer the truth to say that these communities have not so much discovered this approach, but rather unearthed a theology belonging to the early Christian movement. From this they not only see new models of God but also ways in which they can tell of their experiences as a community. So, the community takes responsibility for its experiences and finds a way of describing them. For some ancient communities this may have been told in the form of a song, for others it may have been in the form of a story. Singing the song and telling the story become ways of re-living the experience, but what makes the experience significant is what can be learned from it when the community reflects upon it.

> The theologian . . . must be one who first listens and learns. Practice precedes theoretical systematising; always reality first and reflection later. Reality is the reflected experience of the community.[5]

The local context and use of liberation theology

Despite a relatively recent arrival in Western Europe, liberation theology has been forming in South American history for over a hundred years. It emerged quite publicly at the end of the 1960s as a means of championing the causes of the poor and allowing all oppressed groups and individuals a way of engaging in the

23

political and theological systems of the day.[6] What marks it as quite different from other forms of theology is its very practical nature. It begins not with theory but with action. Because of this it is concerned with the ways that communities express their faith in pastoral care and praxis (practices).

There is a marked contrast between this approach from cultures found in the Southern Hemisphere and with many of those in Western Europe and North America. The latter are sometimes criticised for being overly concerned with orthodoxy (right belief) and with too little concern for orthopraxis (right action). This is a critical distinction. It is the task of every Christian to 'do the work of theology' but too often the tools for doing this work have been so designed that they are unusable by those who have most need of them. The result in Western Europe and North America is that theological reflection as the business of all Christian communities has been effectively neutered.

The production of theological books in these two parts of the world meets the interests of those who are already dominant in the ecclesial and academic systems, a numerically small, academic or clerical/religious readership. Liberation theology recognises this and employs a kind of 'positive discrimination' in the way it tries to work. It owns up to a bias in favour of those groups and individuals that are otherwise fated to remain in these social systems as invisible or 'non persons'. These are the silent voices who are neither strong enough to make themselves heard in the social and ecclesial systems nor empowered within those same systems by the voices already heard. Instead they become the victims of those whose interests are best served by maintaining the current *status quo*. In Africa and Latin America these voices are revealed as those who are economically the most disadvantaged: the poor. In this book they will be seen to be those who are theologically the most disadvantaged if we use only the resources to which academics and clerics have access, namely the language and conceptual understanding of classical theology. The men and women of the congregation at St Luke's are an example of this second disadvantaged group. Their context is clearly not Latin

American, but some of the prejudices and disadvantages they experience may well be equally destructive.

The context of church government

Hierarchically, the Church of England is inclined to be conservative. Ostensibly it would seem that the laity are valued. They have a voice at every level of synodical government, but it would appear that these forums are not as fully representative of lay opinion in the Church as they might be. Because of the way synodical government is designed, the forums have a tendency to attract the verbally articulate and usually the educated middle classes. Ethnic minority groups represented at these forums tend, with some exceptions, to be drawn from the professional classes. At the most local level of church government, the dynamics are the same. Fifteen elected members serve on St Luke's Parochial Church Council. This is the forum for making most of the decisions that concern parish church life. It can deal with anything from deciding matters as mundane as what date is chosen for the Christmas Market to policies concerning the re-marriage of divorcees in church. At almost every meeting between half and two thirds of the members speak in the discussions. They will most often be white professional members, who in the main body of the church are a minority. Clearly the tools for inviting the broadest opinion from within the Church are not the best when they appeal most favourably to one particular social category – already the most advantaged.

The way any church tries to operate will inevitably run up against the problem of bias towards one interest group or another. What needs to be set in place is a system that reveals that bias and allows for the possibility of change.

> Christians often think of the church community as being a place which should be available to, and accepting of, all people, irrespective of their background or social status . . . It is important to remember, however, that for all its rhetoric of inclusion, the institutional church has often been

perceived by the poor and oppressed as being actively on the side of the rich and influential. It is certainly appropriate to try to see the place and position of the church from the perspective of those who have hitherto felt alienated and excluded by it.[7]

Within the wider Church the traditional tools of consultation and discussion on same-sex relationships seem to be more covert in their bias (as I hope will be seen here). This is something that perpetuates the undue influence of one particular group of people. Liberationist technique offers a radical departure from these traditional theological methods. It begins with the experience of the individual and the story of the community, which is why its insights have been used in the collection and collation of raw material for the discussion in this book.

The late Juan Luis Segundo, an early Liberation theologian, devised a four-staged circle for ideas, teachings and traditions to make changes to practical action. The circle begins with the experience of perceived reality. It then compares this experience with the hitherto accepted ideology but in order to do this it uses what it calls a spirit of 'suspicion' as a way of testing the accepted ideology. The next stage sees the community go through a process of reflection and analysis. This is based upon the supposition that in the past the Church (or any other institution) may have given birth to ideas and practices which have consciously or unconsciously created a dynamic of oppressor and oppressed. In its third stage it makes people see the theory in practice and exposes them to the insights and information it has gleaned from the current experience. From doing this it can go onto a fourth stage. It improves the practice according to what it has learned from the reflection. Through this process the community is, in theory, constantly open to both growth and change.

The demographic context

Charlton lies to the south and east of central London. It is situated between the historic and tourist dominated culture of Greenwich, offering the Royal Observatory, the Royal Naval College Museum and the Cutty Sark, and what was industrial Woolwich with its army barracks and armaments factory. Demographically and architecturally, Charlton is a place of contrasts. Despite its capitulation to urban spread (100 years ago it was mostly farmland), many of its original village features remain. The seventeenth-century manor house is the finest example of Jacobean architecture in the United Kingdom. Built originally as a residence for the personal tutor of the Prince of Wales, it now functions as a community centre. There are two village pubs, a cemetery and a parade of shops. The ancient parish church of St Luke is situated at a fork in the road. The original Saxon building probably dates from the twelfth century but was rebuilt in the style of the manor house in 1630. It stands on the brow of a steep hill that descends to the river Thames and for many years was a navigational aid for shipping making their way to the London docks. It is the final resting-place of Spencer Perceval, the only Prime Minister of Great Britain to have been assassinated, and is the spiritual home for the present Christian community of the twenty-first century.

The wider parish of Charlton (beyond the 'village'), remains the home of a top flight Association Football Club (Charlton Athletic) and the world's oldest Rugby Football Club (Blackheath). It has eight schools within it, two sports centres, nine pubs, a health centre and is the home of a newly developed district hospital. These facilities serve a large residential population.

Overall the community has seen dramatic change particularly in the last century. Although Charlton spent most of its life as a small rural village several miles from London, all of this changed at the end of the nineteenth century. The effects of the industrial revolution saw the urban spread of London absorb it. Initially, new industry provided local employment, but that climate has changed significantly since the Second World War and the context is now

27

post-industrial. Many local people travel into the city to work and most of the factories have closed.

However, the preparation for and the passing into a new millennium, have seen some economic resurgence. The building of the Millennium Dome and development of the surrounding area has seen a growth in tourism and generated an increase in property prices. There has been an influx of young professional classes unable to afford property in nearby historic Greenwich. On two sides of the church and manor house the local housing is expensive and owner-occupied. Most of those inhabiting these properties are these same professional classes whose ethnicity is mainly white Anglo-Saxon.

By contrast, stocks of social housing, though still quite high, are becoming increasingly expensive for the local borough council to maintain. On the other two sides of the church are high-rise flats and low-rise, council-owned estates. Many of the tenants are retired, some are unemployed, most are drawn from working-class or unskilled backgrounds, and a large number are from ethnic minority groups including some that have entered the country seeking asylum.

Family models are multifarious. There are a significant number of lone parents, single people living alone, mixed race families and families in which three generations are represented. There are unmarried couples and individuals that move from partner to partner. There are same-gender couples and opposite-gender couples, some with children and some without. Politically the locality is predominantly socialist. All the local ward councillors represent the Labour party, as does the present Member of Parliament. Major problems facing local residents are degrees of soft crime, drugs and racism.

This diversity and change is reflected in the church membership. St Luke's is very much a local community church as most of the adult membership of about 100 live nearby and walk to church. To a large extent the church community is, as you would expect, a reflection of the wider local community. The membership is diverse. There are some from professional classes, a few skilled workers, a number of retired members and some young people who are still at school. Twenty per cent are drawn from ethnic minority groups.

The overwhelming proportion of the church community is on an income of less than £10,000 per annum.

In its recent past the church community has been active in issues of social justice. Newspaper reports in the church archives reveal support for a local family of asylum seekers threatened with deportation, involvement with Third World issues and a serious commitment to supporting those divorced seeking to marry a second time.

During the 1970s and 80s there was strong support for the Movement for the Ordination of Women. This had a particular poignancy as St Luke's had three women on the staff team at the time who were members of the lay order of deaconesses and who wanted to have their vocations tested as priests. One (Liz Canham) eventually went to live in the USA and became the first Anglican English-woman to be ordained to the priesthood.

The archives also document the church's support for gay and lesbian couples wanting their relationships affirmed by the Church and recognised by law. A more detailed background follows in the next chapter.

Supporting such causes and perceiving them to be issues of social justice has given the church members a strong sense of their need for each other. There is a strong sense of 'togetherness', which is reflected in the comments of visitors who often describe it as a genuinely friendly community. This is a church community well suited to the practical, 'liberationist' kind of theological reflection and to lifestyles that are defined not primarily by ideology but by practices, that is with a bias to right living or right practice rather than what some perceive to be right believing.[8]

In turn this strong sense of community has allowed a style of local church decision-making to emerge that is collaborative. The laity lead parts of the Sunday worship: they are responsible for readings, prayers and administering the Holy Communion. The laity choose the music for worship each week without the supervision of the clergy. They are participants in changes to current liturgical practices and the creation of new ones. They organise the strategies to encourage regular financial giving and take responsibility for other stewardship initiatives. Despite the apparent weaknesses of the local church government system, the laity do at least get to elect representatives each year to the PCC. This is a group that influences much that drives local church life. So what we have is a contextual picture that sees the decision-making processes at a local level seeming to operate on a relatively level playing field.

> There is a fundamental equality in the Church. All are People of God. All share in Christ, directly and without mediation. Therefore, all share in the services of teaching, sanctifying and organising the community. All are sent out on a mission; all are responsible for the unity of the community; all must be sanctified.[9]

If the unity of a church community is, to some extent, dependant upon that community's willingness to take responsibility for its ordering, worship, teaching and mission, then that responsibility extends to its pastoral action too. Churches need to discover ways of reflecting on the things they do and how the people they serve receive them. The liberation theology method is not the only way, but it is one that I have borrowed features of to allow this particular congregation to think about its attitudes towards gay and lesbian couples.

The national church context

In moving from the local church context to that of the national church we find similarities, but enormous differences too. At a national level, decisions are made through a hierarchical layer of synodical government. Ironically the most localised of these (the Deanery Synod) has no power to make policy for the local group of churches it represents. Thus there is little incentive to participate in them. My own experience has been one in which such synods are rarely fully represented and attendance levels are often poor.

The Diocesan Synods are the next layer of government. They feed the National forum called the General Synod, which is the main policy-making body. Naturally, both these layers attract those who are most able to use the debating forum as already described. However, participation in the General Synod inadvertently discriminates against the economically disadvantaged. If you are employed you need to be able to afford to take time off work to attend the sessions.

Historically General Synod has proved to have a chameleon character. On matters of social justice it has adopted quite radical positions. Its report on nuclear weapons and urban regeneration had far-reaching effects, made waves for the Government of the day and drew unpopular criticism from Conservative Members of Parliament.[10] However, on issues concerning sexuality, it tends to lean in a very conservative direction. It is as divided as any other part of the Church or institution caring to offer opinions on gay and lesbian relationships. This has often been revealed in some of the bitter discussions that have taken place.

In 1979 the Church of England issued its first report on same-sex relationships. Called the *Gloucester Report*, it set out how same-sex relationships might be received and fostered within the Christian life. The report sought permanence, faithfulness and stability for same-sex couples and urged the Church to recognise gay relationships. The report was received but never officially ratified.

In 1987 the General Synod of the Church of England debated the status of same-sex relationships. The mood of the debate was heated and at times acrimonious. Far from accepting the position suggested by the compilers of the *Gloucester Report*, they concentrated on 'acts' rather than relationships and managed to conclude that 'homosexual acts fall short of the ideal'. One observer was prompted to write:

> One of the wiser things that Archbishop Runcie said in the infamous Higton debate of 1987 was that, 'In this earthly

31

tabernacle of Christ's kingdom there are many mansions and all of them are made of glass'. The truth is that in all matters of human relationship, heterosexual or homosexual we all 'fall short' of the ideal.[11]

The anxiety felt in the aftermath of the 1987 General Synod debate might have had some bearing on two succeeding events.

The first was the Lambeth Conference of 1988. This conference, held once every ten years, is an opportunity for all the bishops in the Anglican Communion to exchange ideas, discuss global issues of common interest and to share the problems of the Church in different parts of the world. Two significant things emerged in the discussions on human sexuality. The first was that, after the discussions surrounding gay and lesbian relationships, no vote was taken. The conference saw itself as in no position to make any kind of authoritative declaration. Experience of and attitudes towards homosexuality were relative to culture and context. An African bishop would bring to the discussion a culturally formed attitude and experience that would be quite different from an American bishop.

The second significant discussion at this Lambeth Conference was of polygamy. The African bishops appealed to the conference for openness in understanding the multifarious contexts of the African situation. The conference did. Polygamous marriages were recognised as something that had been shaped by social and political culture and context. This was a significant step in responding to a pastoral dilemma in certain parts of the Communion. It openly asserted that culture and context do make a difference when determining adequate pastoral responses. It recognised in this that there were some issues for which such a conference simply could not legislate. This was a critical insight into the nature of the conference itself and how it might approach the entire subject of human sexuality.

The Lambeth Conference of 1998 seemed to have forgotten this insight. A thoughtful paper written jointly by Bishop Jack Spong of Newark (USA) and Bishop Peter John Lee of Christ the King

(South Africa) was published prior to the conference. They called it 'A Catechesis on Homosexuality'[12] and defined catechesis as 'A dialogue between believers'. In it they noted firstly their points of agreement: human life is sacred, marriage and family life important and promiscuous or predatory sexual behaviour is dehumanising and wrong.[13] Secondly they noted three further areas on which they could not find agreement at that time. This included the blessing of same-sex couples, the ordination to the priesthood of gay and lesbian people in faithful monogamous relationships and the authority of the Bible.[14] They suggested that no vote be taken on blessing same-gender unions and the ordination of gay men and lesbian women in active monogamous partnerships. Instead they recognised that this was an issue that the Church was still actively discerning and that taking a vote might prove to be destructive.

> If the Lambeth Conference debates these three conflicted issues and forces a vote one way or the other the result will be bitterness, and surely a minority report will be issued by the losing side.[15]

Their suggestion was ignored.

Major national newspapers, anticipating a bloodbath of disagreement, filled their columns the next day with accounts of a debate and a vote that was indeed bitter, and damaging.

> *How I felt the wrath of a bishop . . . as the Church*
> *votes for gay ban*
> The hours leading up to the vote saw scenes of unprecedented vitriol, near violence . . .[16]

> *Bishops plot against 'pathetic' Carey in*
> *gay vote backlash*
> One bishop walked out of the session saying it had made him feel 'physically sick'; a leading American liberal bishop caused uproar when he described African church leaders as 'superstitious'. One bishop said the centrepiece debate on

homosexuality 'had a violent tone which was very distressing –
barracking and laughter by the victors . . .' Observers were
amazed by the dissention within Anglican ranks.[17]

Liberal bishops lose the war of words

The first minutes of the debate were devoted to calming
tempers and soothing the African bishops who had
threatened to walk out if any concession was made to the
liberals.[18]

Anti-gay bishops crush liberals

Outside the hall there were bitter confrontations between
advocates of gay rights and opponents. The Rt Rev
Emmanuel Chukwuma, Bishop of Enugu, Nigeria tried to
'cure' Richard Kirker, spokesman of the Lesbian and Gay
Christian Movement, by laying on hands. 'Repent of your
sin. You have no inheritance in the Kingdom of God. Your
Church is dying in Europe because you condone immorality.
You have made yourselves homosexuals because of your
carnality,' he told him.[19]

The debate continued for more than two hours during which
the bishops added five amendments to the original resolution and
eventually voted on a motion that was considerably more conservative than it had been at the outset. In it they declared that:

> The conference cannot advise the legitimising or blessing
> of same-sex unions or ordaining of those involved in such
> unions.

Of the 739 bishops attending the conference, 641 took part in this
debate. 526 voted in favour of the resolution, 70 against and 45
abstained.

The second significant event, alongside the Lambeth Confer-
ences, was the publication of the report *Issues in Human Sexuality*[20]
by the House of Bishops of the Church of England. It appeared in
1991 as a discussion document. The Archbishop of Canterbury,
George Carey, in his introduction warmly commends it for dis-

cussion at all levels of the Church and is very clear that the House of Bishops understood this to be a statement 'which we do not pretend to be the last word on the subject'.[21]

However, if it began life purporting to be a 'discussion' document, it now seems, in practice, to have acquired a different status in certain quarters. Stories abound of Church leaders using it as a policy document for determining the suitability of candidates for ordination or the granting of licenses to clergy. Newly appointed bishops, when asked their view on ordaining clergy in same-sex partnerships, would often declare themselves to be in line with the bishops' statement in *Issues in Human Sexuality*. It is difficult to gauge exactly how much discussion the document has provoked at a local level and yet it was a resolution of the 1988 Lambeth Conference that called on the bishops of the Anglican Communion to spend time in the next ten years in a 'Deep and dispassionate study of the question of homosexuality.'[22]

The document has its positive points. For the first time, the bishops encouraged the Church to offer a positive welcome to gay and lesbian people. They affirmed faithful same-sex relationships and described them as a 'blessing' in some instances to those around them. But the document lacks congruity. It tells the reader that while faithful partnerships may be a good thing, they are not recommended for the clergy. It says that this is because the clergy have

> a distinct calling, nature and consecration any claim to such partnerships would be misread as placing same-sex partnerships on a par with heterosexual marriage as a reflection of God's purposes in creation.[23]

This would appear to imply that those who are not clergy, who nonetheless live in faithful same-sex partnerships, would not cause any such misreading. This seems to be an illogical nonsense. The muddle exists because the document has multiple authors. This could have been a real strength, but instead is its weakness.

The document has been called a 'holding operation'.[24] The one thing that is clear is that its theology does not hang together. It is unable to point to a cohesive solution, hardly surprising since it is rumoured that the document was originally written with more than one conclusion for pastoral action! If this is so then as a pastoral document it is a sham.

The truth is that it is difficult for the leaders of any Church to offer a pastoral document written for discussion in the way that *Issues in Human Sexuality* has been written. Both Lambeth 1998 and this document reveal an anxious attempt to show a united front. Lambeth failed in that attempt because it showed a greater pre-occupation with 'winning the argument' than with engaging in a process of sensitive listening. *Issues* failed because it tried to be all things to all people. Furthermore, neither the conference nor the book contains the voices of the Church's laity. The conference was not open to the voices of gay and lesbian people. That has not stopped some bishops adopting *Issues* and the resolutions of Lambeth 1998 as the benchmark for church discipline. On matters concerning same-sex relationships and the admission to holy orders of men and women who are pursuing active same-gender partnerships, for some they have even acquired a regulatory status.

Given that General Synod has never ratified *Issues*, and that the Lambeth Conference has never been accorded the status of a synod, I would suggest that however unwittingly these misperceptions have been conveyed, they are very worrying.

The secular context

What Lambeth 1998 revealed was that if context is to be taken seriously, an international discussion on the issues surrounding the status of gay and lesbian partnerships is virtually impossible. The widely contrasting experiences of each bishop in his or her social situation and the impact of that experience upon the life of that part of the global Church were so varied that in conference they seemed to find little common ground. This book will report the unheard voices at the baseline of the Church, the voices of those who experience the Church's ministry to them, and will draw on some of those influences and experiences already described.

Andrew Sullivan offers a good description of attitudes to gay men and lesbian women in a North American cultural context.[25] Many of his insights can be found in parts of Western Europe too. He defines society's responses to homosexual relationships in general within four categories. These he calls the 'prohibitionist', 'liberationist', 'conservative' and 'liberal' positions. What he describes in most if not all of these positions can also be found within the Church, revealing it as a microcosm of the wider societal context that it reflects. This makes the debate about human sexuality in general and homosexuality in particular an important one for the Church to have at all levels.

Sullivan describes a societal scene created by us through a combination of fear and ignorance. It is a climate that bears all the marks of repression and has invited a two-fold response among many gay men and lesbian women. The choice is fight or flight, campaign or hide.

> It's no wonder, perhaps that male homosexual culture has developed an ethic more of anonymous or promiscuous sex than of committed relationships.[26]

Much of this is made worse by so many different reactions from so many parts of society.

The first attitude to same-gender relationships is what Sullivan calls *prohibitionist*: the view that the homosexual nature is a 'condition' described in negative and alienating language. Being gay is referred to as 'abhorrent' and an 'abomination'. The response to it is largely punitive.

Those within the Church who hold this view are those who advocate the removal of openly gay and lesbian clergy from their livings and the withholding of ordination from homophile people who will not declare themselves to be celibate. Many occupy the wings of Christian fundamentalism, either in sects or in extreme pressure groups within the national Church. The latter have been seen to deny their bishops welcome access to the parish church and to preside at the sacraments in that church unless the bishops subscribe to the same view of gay and lesbian people that they themselves hold. The more compassionate of those in this category see the homosexual condition as one that might be altered through what they will describe as 'healing' ministries, claiming that through psychotherapeutic engagement and prayer, homophile behaviour can be 'corrected'.[27]

> The most humane representatives of this view seek to bring people trapped in homosexual behaviour back into con-formity with what they see as their natural, their true calling, and re-envelop them in a meaningful and constructive human community.[28]

Those outside the Church holding this prohibitionist perspective deem that society should legislate and enforce legal punishments. To them normality is the way of the heterosexual majority and only that norm should be allowed.

The second category contains those that Sullivan calls *liberationist*. This is a term used elsewhere in this book to denote a way of doing theology. It should not be confused with the sense in which it is used in this descriptive analysis. Those adopting the Sullivan liberationist perspective see the homosexual 'condition' as a construct of human thought generated by the powerful to control the powerless. What this means is that the liberationists sees themselves as the counter-culture movement to all other groups and the prohibitionists in particular. For the liberationist the task is to be free of all such constraints in order to come into a fully formed identity chosen by the individual. 'Outing' gay individuals is part of the liberationist ethos because it purports to challenge the boundaries of 'public' and 'private'. Groups like 'Outrage' take this view. Ironically, the deployment of such extreme tactics seems to do little to empower or liberate the oppressed individual. Instead the so-called liberationist just compounds a stereotype of gays and lesbians, one that depicts them either as immature anarchists or as unstable predators and bullies who select 'soft' targets like the Church to vent their anger on. From this perspective same-sex blessings are nothing but a sell-out, an abject copy of what society is used to: marriage between hetero-sexuals.[29]

The third viewpoint is described as *conservative*. This view espouses civil liberties but affirms certain cultural, social and moral values over others. Homosexual people exist and in *conservative* opinion (off the record) they have a right to live free of harassment, violence and ill-treatment. However this private tolerance is often matched with public disapproval.

> While they do not want to see legal persecution of homo-sexuals, they see no problem with discouragement and disparagement of homosexual sexual behaviour in the abstract, or more commonly, a carefully sustained hush on the matter altogether.[30]

Those holding this view of homosexuality seem to centre their thinking on sexual activity. They see all sexual activity as being designed exclusively for procreation, which can, therefore, occur only within the institution of marriage between heterosexuals. Within the Church these conservatives declare that the blessing of same-gender partnerships somehow diminishes the institution of marriage. Either it is perceived to be a mockery of marriage (and therefore of a valid form of heterosexual life), or it is seen as undermining. Conservatives will often balk at publicly acknowl-edging same-gender partnerships for fear of being seen to place them on a 'par' with heterosexual marriage. Furthermore, active encouragement of alternative styles of relationship is seen as weak-ening the stability of family life and encouraging 'waverers' towards a lifestyle that is self-destructive. The problem with the conservative view is that it does nothing to provide social or familial support for same-sex couples. It does not allow the de-velopment of institutions or frameworks that encourage same-sex fidelity or monogamy. Ironically this seems to run counter to the rest of the perceived conservative social agenda.

The real danger here lies in the perception of dual standards. On the one hand it is recognised that stability in relationships is a foundation stone for societies built on the values of the

conservative perspective. On the other, conservatives seem paralysed to do anything positive about it, preferring instead to keep
as quiet as possible in the hope that the matter will resolve itself.

On the political frontier, some are beginning to move. Conservative Members of Parliament as a rule tend to fall into the
conservative category. However, some are now prepared to break
rank, noting that at a fundamental level, gay and lesbian couples
do not have equal standing in society. Some ministers perceive this
as a form of discrimination not dissimilar to that of institutional
racism. However, even they will only go as far as describing their
support for gays and lesbians to 'register' their partnerships. The
language of marriage remains under careful wraps.[31]

Sullivan argues that it should be perfectly possible to combine
a celebration of the traditional family with the celebration of a
stable homosexual relationship.

> . . . the notion of stable gay relationships might even serve
> to buttress the ethic of heterosexual marriage, by showing
> how even those excluded from it can wish to model them-
> selves on its shape and structure.[32]

Given that this is precisely the *status quo* that the so-called liberationists seek to overthrow it is hard to see why it receives no
open support from those of a more conservative persuasion. The
result is a confused social climate in which tolerance seems to be
encouraged while publicly denied. This tips homosexuality into
two different domains; public and private. In the modern European
and North American context these two faces have existed for a
long time and yet many now perceive them to be least tenable.
Two things in particular have seen to this: the emergence of the
AIDS/HIV issue and the debate about homosexuality within
the armed services. Those holding a conservative position within
the Church continue to exercise what they regard as 'discretion'.
They don't ask the questions that they don't want answers for.

The fourth viewpoint is the *liberal* perspective. Most of us deploy
at least an aspect of liberalism, but few will admit to a liberal
persuasion. Liberalism has been reduced by a skilful propaganda

to something resembling an insult. Within the Church, liberalism is portrayed as the bringer of uncertainty. Liberals are depicted as doubters of everything, loose in their theological thinking and generally 'unsound'. They stand accused as those for whom, in credo and praxis, anything goes. Some evangelicals distance them-selves from the name of liberalism, preferring instead to describe themselves as 'open' rather than liberal. Prohibitionists demonise liberals, creating an air of suspicion around them and leaving the liberal position uncomfortable. For some this is because in supporting the rights of gay and lesbian couples there are, as they see it, costs to the rest of society, which liberals either overlook or deny. They take the position that if there is to be recognition of same-gender couples and a way of legitimising their partnerships, it will either validate a lifestyle that they cannot find in Scripture or tradition, or else it completely redefines what they regard as 'normal'. This is a cost that they are reluctant to meet and one that they are resentful of bearing on what they perceive to be a liberal 'whim.'

Whatever the reason, it seems clear that, without the liberal contribution there would have been no debate at all. However, liberals have been guilty of major neglect in the area of public rights. It is one thing to see the need for change in personal attitudes, which liberalism does well. It is something else to see gay men and lesbian women given public equality. That is precisely what some gay and lesbian couples are calling for. It is something that others take for granted.

> Imagine life without a recognised family; imagine dating without even the possibility of marriage. Any heterosexual woman who can imagine being told at a young age that her attraction to men was wrong, that her loves and crushes were illicit, that her destiny were singlehood and shame, will also appreciate the point. Gay marriage is not a radical step; it is a profoundly humanising, traditionalising step. It is the first step in any resolution of the homosexual question — more important than any other institution, since it is the

most central institution to the nature of the problem, which is to say, the emotional and sexual bond between one human being and another.[33]

In response to this, we now turn to listen to the unheard voices.

CHAPTER 3

Unheard Voices

a story remembered

In the opening chapter of her book *Women around Jesus*, Elisabeth Moltmann tells the story of a base community in Latin America.[1] These communities are small gatherings of Christians, often meeting to discuss how the gospels link with life and the struggle for liberation. In this particular story, a group of men and women meet for discussion with their priest. They discuss the resurrection narratives in the gospels.

As the discussion begins it is noted that it is the women who go to the tomb to attend to the body of Jesus. The men who have been his high-profile followers are in hiding because they are afraid. The women in the discussion group become quite animated at this point and begin to speak in excited voices, saying that it is the women of the story who have real courage. They are not afraid, but then, they say, women are like that, they do not fear, they are stronger than men are. The men in the group now begin to grumble and murmur their disapproval. Women are not braver than men are and in any event what was so brave about going to visit a grave? It was not the magnanimous gesture they, the women, were trying to make it seem. The priest (who is, of course, male) now intervenes with his theological contribution. An analysis of culture and context, he tells the group, would have revealed that it was safer for women to go to the tomb than for men. Their low social standing meant that any evidence they offered of an empty grave and a resurrection message would carry no weight in religious or societal law, simply because they were women. The women in the discussion group fall silent.

Moltmann uses this illustration to make a serious point: that men have always silenced women's voices. The recounting of history has been told almost exclusively through the voices of men. Her book goes on to explore ways of discovering the life stories of the women who followed Jesus in the early Christian movement.

Her insight was important in the decision to collect material for this book. In every church community there are voices that never seem to get heard. As we have already seen in Chapter Two, the systems we deploy to share power and make decisions are often seen to favour one group and disadvantage others. So, in collecting the research material it was important to note these insights and to listen to a wide variety of people to create as even-handed an approach as possible. This will be described later.

From the silencing of the women in Moltmann's story we see how easily important perspectives can be suppressed. The women perceive courage in the women of the gospel – a courage that is, for them, identified with universal womankind. It is as they become more involved in the story that their voices are silenced by loud resentment from their menfolk and the rational analytical contribution of their priest. Their way of telling the story never gets another chance.

The power of story

A friend once told me of an experience of story-telling in South Africa. The community he was staying with had invited him to join their evening gathering. He recalls members of the village assembling to hear a young boy telling a story. He was unable to understand the words of the story because he was unfamiliar with the local dialect but as the story unfolded, the boy's facial actions and body language absorbed him. The boy told the story not just with the words, but with his whole self. Furthermore, as the story progressed, all the listeners began to engage, first through silent absorption and then with laughter and cheering. The power of the story was in the way it was told and in the way it belonged to the whole community.

Many of the insights brought to us by the work of liberation theology come through the power of story-telling. Western European and North American cultures are learning to use story-telling in a similar way. In a culture that has seen story-telling operate almost solely at the level of entertainment, it has left some with the perception that story-telling is the same as 'telling stories', or relaying fiction. This over-emphasis on stories as entertainment has diminished the power of story-telling as a vehicle for conveying insights about human life.

Fortunately there are signs of recovery. Stories and story-telling are re-emerging in Western Europe and North America as valued ways and means of conveying significant insights about human life. Some have even spilled into the world of academic theology. Amongst theological writers from these cultures James Hopewell is one who pleads a strong case for the power of story in congregational analysis.[2] In *Congregation: Stories and Structure*, his major life-work on the formation of congregations, Hopewell argues that people looking for a church community to belong to do not attach themselves to congregations in an *ad hoc* fashion. Each will be attracted to a community that itself has a story with which the individual can identify or which fits with their own human life story.

> Story is a device by which perceptions of corporate life are arranged in a telling way, but that is not their first or only function. Story is also the form by which corporate experience is in the first instance perceived.[3]

If Hopewell is right then it is only when a community begins to *tell* its story that that community comes to understand something of its identity, nature and mission. Allowing communities to reflect on their pastoral practice in this way is bound to have significance for more than just the local community itself. If this theory of story-telling proves true, then in telling its story any local church community will not only reveal how it sees itself in the larger parish community, but it is likely to make impact at other levels of the Church as well. The power of story-telling then lies in enabling a community to exert influence beyond itself.

Whether this theory proves to be true in this instance remains to be seen. The reader can decide whether this particular congregation, by telling its story, has made connections or not. Our task was not, in the first instance, to form a world-view or come to conclusions about gay and lesbian relationships in society. Instead we have attempted to remember and tell a part of our own story and look at how that has bearing on our views and feelings about same-gender partnerships today. That is the principal task. If other congregations feel encouraged to follow suit either with regard to gay and lesbian lifestyles or to any other feature of pastoral ministry, then that is to be welcomed.

Method and structure

The people at St Luke's church have, for 20 years, declared their support for gay and lesbian couples and have asked their clergy to bless, where they felt appropriate, their unions. There were, however, some dissenting voices amongst the general assent. We therefore allowed a genuine cross-section of members of the congregation to contribute their experiences, from events leading to the original decision to support such pastoral practices to the long-term effect of that decision on the community. This would allow their own story to be told with their own voices.

Furthermore, it was agreed that the couples who had come to St Luke's in search of blessing and support should be given the opportunity to tell their story too.

This chapter looks at the beginning of the story as told by members of the local church. The voices of gay and lesbian couples are found in Chapter Four.

Five selected members of the congregation conducted the interviews. One other member of the congregation supervised these and reported their findings to me. I interviewed all the couples who took part. They provided a representative sample of the couples who had experienced services of blessing over an eight-year period. The interviews with both church members and couples were all tape recorded and subsequently transcribed. All participants who so wished were granted anonymity.

The interviewees were chosen at random according to agreed categories. Their names were quite literally drawn out of a hat! The categories were determined by the length of time spent in membership at St Luke's along with two other special categories.

Category one was a sample of people who had been members for 15 years or more, the Senior members. Category two was the Intermediates, those who had been members for between five and 15 years. Category three, the Newcomers, was a sample of those who had been members for five years or less.

The two other categories were of voices that are often unheard in the church community, hence the special attention. The first was those whose ethnicity could be defined as black or coloured African/Caribbean. Such members make up nearly 20 per cent of the congregation and are often under-represented in church life. The second was that of young people, some of whom would not even be recorded on the church membership roll because they were less than 16 years of age. It was agreed to enlist a group of 13- to 18-year-olds for interview with the consent of their parents.

In the final section of this chapter I am interested in discovering what each member of the church congregation knew about the story of Rodney Madden and Saxon Lucas. How that story is passed on, or not, and which parts of the congregation gather that story into the overall church story should provide a platform for assessing attitudes towards the blessing of same-sex relationships then and now. Matters concerning the nature of blessing, theology and practice are all considered in subsequent chapters. Recommendations for future 'good practice' are found in Appendix A, thus completing the circle/spiral technique borrowed from the base community world of Latin America and adapted for use in the context of the local church community here. A liturgy of blessing devised by members of the congregation adopting the insights of their reflection will be found in Appendix B.

The church members

In order to make easier reading, those interviewed have been placed in the categories of church membership described earlier. Some names have been changed.

Category (C1) Senior members (15+ years membership)

James is 91 years old and recently widowed. He moved to Charlton during the Second World War where he taught in a local polytechnic, eventually becoming head of his department. He and his late wife brought their family up at St Luke's and he has been a member for more than 55 years.

Millie is 73 years old. She has been twice widowed, is a mother and grandmother and during her professional working life was a private secretary for 20 years before becoming a cost accountant. She has been an active member of St Luke's for 16 years.

Jennifer is 74 and single. She is a retired Civil Servant having spent most of her career in the Diplomatic Service. Her membership is a little more than 25 years standing.

Doreen is 80 years old and widowed. She was formerly a carer for her mother and latterly for her husband. She has been a member of St Luke's for 20 years.

Lavinia is 70 years old and is divorced. In her working career she was a Chief Scientific Officer in a medical research unit. She has been a member at the church for just over 30 years.

Category (C2) Intermediate members (5–15 years membership)

Moira is 56 years old and single. She describes her work as secretarial and something that takes her abroad a lot. This means that she has lived in a number of different countries. She first joined St Luke's 29 years ago but is included in this category since she most recently returned to the United Kingdom just over six years ago.

June is 64 years old and single. She is a retired bank official where she worked as a project manager. She is now on the church stewardship team and is involved with the local Sea Rangers. June has been at the church for 15 years.

Mary is a middle-aged former midwife. Married, with two grown-up children, she works professionally on a part-time basis. She has been at St Luke's for 15 years where she sings in the church choir.

Arthur is 55 years old and single. He lives alone and works as an engineering draughtsman in an industry that has become quite run down. He has been made redundant five times and his current job is under threat, making life quite stressful. He has been a member of St Luke's for 15 years and is an altar server.

Sally is a middle-aged woman with grown-up children. She is interested in and involves herself with local community issues.

Category (C3) Recent members (0–5 years membership)

Sara was born in the United States of America but has now made her home in the United Kingdom. She is in her forties, is self-employed and has two children of school age. She has been a member of the church for between four and five years.

Daisy describes herself as a former schoolteacher in her mid-fifties. She is married with two grown-up children and has been a member of St Luke's for about five years.

Roger is in his late thirties and is married. After living abroad for some years he returned to Britain and came to live in the parish. He is an architect and has a growing London-based business. He has been a member of the church for about three years.

Nathaniel is in his early thirties and is an experienced manager with voluntary organisations. He is currently a student and has been a member of the church for about five years.

Edna and Wally are husband and wife both in their seventies. They have one adult son. Wally is a retired engineer. Edna has battled with cancer for ten years. They have been members of St Luke's for five years. Edna died six months after taking part in the research for this book.

Category (C4) Membership representing ethnic minority groups

Brenda was born in Ghana. She is married and is a mother, grand-mother and great-grandmother. She describes herself as 'retired' and has been a member of St Luke's for 30 years, where she is a member of the team welcoming worshippers to Sunday worship.

Tina was born in Jamaica and is a former schoolteacher. She is in her mid-fifties, divorced and mother of three children. She works as a professional carer employed by the local authority. At church she is part of the welcome team and is on the Scripture reading rota. She has been a member of St Luke's for 17 years.

Sandra was born in Jamaica and came to the United Kingdom as a teenager where she began training as a nurse. She is divorced with children and grandchildren and latterly cared for her elderly mother who died two years ago. She has been a church member at St Luke's for 19 years.

Sharon was also born in Jamaica. She is a retired hospital worker who has been a member at St Luke's for five years. She is divorced, a mother and grandmother.

Penny was born in Ghana. She is divorced with children and grandchildren and worked for a number of years as a secretary in the Civil Service. She is a volunteer visitor at the local hospital. She is a church representative on the diocesan black forum. She joined St Luke's 15 years ago. On Sundays she sometimes reads the lesson, leads prayers and helps distribute communion.

Category (C5) Membership representing young people

Alex is 14 years old. He likes sport and plays rugby for his school. He plays guitar and enjoys all forms of music. He has attended St Luke's with his parents since birth where he is now an altar server and member of the youth group.

Daniel is 16 and has left school to attend a day college to do computer studies. He is a member of the Air Training Corps, a helper with the church Beaver Colony and an altar server. He was baptised at St Luke's as a baby and has attended with his mother throughout his childhood and adolescence.

Eddy is 14 years old. At school he is beginning to get ready for his GCSE's where his favourite subjects are information technology and drama. He is a keen supporter of Charlton Football Club, is an altar server and member of the youth group. He has attended the church with his parents since he was eight years old.

Emily is 18 years old. After leaving school she worked in a solicitor's office before beginning her training to be a Nursery Nurse. She is an altar server and keen participant in occasional church amateur dramatics. She has been coming to church with her grandmother since she was six.

Nicola is 18 years old and is studying for 'A' levels. She likes salsa dancing and competes at tournaments. She has attended St Luke's with her family since she was four years old.

Tom is in his first year of senior school where he enjoys football and rugby. He is interested in computers, likes reading and outdoor activities. He is an altar server and helps out on church quiz nights. He has been coming to St Luke's with his family from the time he was born.

Reflection on belonging and relationship

Why people choose to live in communities is partly determined by the human need to belong. The church members began by considering the nature of belonging and to what extent we are all defined by our relationships. Nearly everyone taking part saw belonging as something to do with identification. Who I am and how I identify what it is that I am becoming as I grow to mature adulthood has something to do with where I choose to locate myself.

Seeing the Church as a community of homebuilders
James Hopewell's theory materialises quickly, namely that individuals find their way to churches where the images of the

church story link up with the stories of each individual. The interviewees' first task was to describe how they see themselves when, as different sections of the congregation, they gather as St Luke's church. This is significant since the way a community sees itself will have a bearing upon the way it conducts itself not only in worship but also in what it determines to be pastoral care. This in turn will influence those drawn to it, either as potential members, or in need of that care, or both.

Seeing the Church as mother

For those in the ethnic minority category, for example, there was an important sense of what it meant to be an Anglican Christian. This was much more strongly defined than in any other category. Many represented in this category are first generation African or West Indian now relocated in England. They bring a culture of churchgoing learned in their country of birth. They were Anglicans then and there is no question that they will be anything else now.

> I was born into our church, which was in Ghana. I was baptised and confirmed an Anglican. When I came here with my husband all my life I was with St Luke's. We came here from Cornwall and I started looking for the Anglican church. *(Brenda, C4)*

> I am an Anglican so wherever I go I look for an Anglican church to attend. *(Penny, C4)*

For many African-Caribbean Anglicans, Church is 'mother' who feeds, teaches, disciplines and inspires loyalty and obedience. For some African and West Indian Christians an attachment of this kind is a connection with 'home' and a desire to treat this as a piece of 'home' from the past in a country they are currently making their home. Finding home in a country that might not be the country of birth and upbringing suggests that there is something comforting in the familiar. It brings with it a picture of family with mother at the centre always knowing what to do next, what advice to give and what nourishment to serve up.

Seeing the Church as a community of sanctuary

A second model of Church was identified most strongly amongst the most senior members. The sense of Church as home, and home as a place of safety developed into a model of Church we might describe as 'sanctuary'.

Most of these members had undergone a specific search for a place of safety that felt like home. Each of them describes a unique set of personal circumstances. One found her way because of a death in the family and was met with kindness in the church community at a time of grief and loss. Another described a period 30 years before when her life had reached a critical moment. Those who had helped her the most were integral members of the church community at St Luke's. Lavinia described herself as having been solidly atheistic for a large period of her life. What she identified about the life of community in St Luke's was something very close to sanctuary at a time of crisis. In danger it is quite natural to gravitate towards people and places of safety, which is what she did.

> It seemed as if it was a very natural place to . . . I suppose something I was looking for. Needing care, which I got in bucket loads, it felt like coming home . . . it just felt right from day one. *(Lavinia, C1)*

Interestingly, there were people in every category who saw Church as sanctuary. While some came looking for a church to meet a particular need, others described St Luke's as sanctuary because of the make up of the congregation. Sanctuary came to be seen as a place that crosses bridges of class and culture. The desire for sanctuary, or the need to feel safe, is then not so much about finding yourself with people of similar circumstance, it is more to do with finding friendship and acceptance in a place where real difference exists and nobody minds.

Seeing the Church as a community of friends living with diversity

The theme of diversity emerged rapidly in the interviews. Whereas stability and safety are often equated with like-mindedness and the capacity to find agreement, the members describe a pattern of stability found precisely in their own patterns of diversity. They all seem to be aware that they have differences and that they live alongside others that hold views at variance with their own.

All church communities have differences and manage them with varying degrees of success, but issues around gender and sexuality seem to be among the most combustible. Can any church community live with the differences that will almost certainly emerge from reflecting upon their ministry to same-gender couples, and still remain in full community with each other?

Members of St Luke's seem to see as an obvious strength that their church draws the bulk of its membership from the wider local community rather than an eclectic congregation that travel great distances to worship week by week because they like the music or the architecture or the preacher. So what emerged from some of those interviewed was a picture of their church as an extraordinary place precisely because of its ordinariness. It seems to blend in well with the surrounding area and is a fair representation of the demographic context in which it is to be found.

> It is a friendly congregation and you can meet anybody and everybody who is part of the community of Charlton. That is why we are happy to stay . . . If there are things that are not your favourite things then you can live with them and try to influence them. At the end of the day you just remain part of the village. *(Mary, C2)*

One aspect of local life (what Mary calls 'village'), is to reckon on being different and holding different views. What is important for Mary is to remain part of that. If the local church is to be seen as a microcosm of the local community then perhaps the way in which we have differences is also part of what it means to be

'Church'. Certainly Mary is committed to staying with differences if only to influence change.

It is likely that her view is one that represents a significant number of voices across the entire congregation. It is interesting to compare her view with that of Arthur. She and he will emerge as diametrically opposed in their views on same-gender unions, but their reasons for living alongside one another in that community of diversity are remarkably similar.

> It's all the fault of Norman Vincent Peel, the Doctor of Divinity, having read his book on the power of positive thinking. In it he laid down the theory that no one is complete unless they go to church . . . I came to St Luke's because it was the nearest church. As the years have gone by my views have changed dramatically in all sorts of ways . . .
> *(Arthur, C2)*

Arthur, as part of his search for completeness, is influenced by the idea of positive thinking. For this he is prepared to remain within a community that has others holding views quite different from his own and he acknowledges that sometimes this has brought about change in him. It is as though he and Mary are each prepared to be part of a community that can influence change and be influenced by it. They disagree with each other and yet they are committed to staying in community with each other because, ironically, they see themselves and their community grow through enabling change. Often we count as our friends those with whom we have significant agreement and find common ground. Here is a model of friendship that exists to foster positive attitudes in agreeing to differ. Later we will see friendship as a significant feature of not only community life but also within intimate partnerships.

Seeing the Church as a community of empowerment

If churches are serious about addressing the tensions of living with differences then they must look at the way they handle power within their structures. 'Power' and 'empowerment' are fashionable; almost jargon words that are often deemed to be the preserve of the Politically Correct. Churches, like other organisations, have power dynamics at every level. To those on the inside these seem benign to the point of non-existence, but to those who are outside the accredited membership they are stark and sometimes disabling. So, for someone entering a church for the first time, the strange ceremonials, the language, music and observance of ritual and local custom is a disadvantage. For some it can be an uncomfortable experience. This can be seen too in the ways that people approach their local church for pastoral care. Most arrive in a position of vulnerability. They may be bereaved, or feeling guilty about something said or done. They may need affirmation or encouragement, but fear the possibilities of rejection or judgement. Those dispensing pastoral care in these situations are in a powerful position. Positive use of power and influence can make a church community seem quite attractive. When questioned why they had chosen to join this particular local church, it was those church members who had experienced positive pastoral care in times of crisis or need who were able to describe this most effectively. Jennifer (C1) joined because the curate was kind to her when her mother died. Lavinia (C1) came along following a personal crisis and found that people had time for her. Edna (C3) made her way into church at a time of serious illness and found people who would listen to her. All of them found a positive response during a critical period of their lives.

Sara (C3) came to church, not because of a pastoral crisis, but because her child wanted to come. She said that the kind of welcome she received allowed her sufficient space to find her own way into the church community. Acceptance and empowerment have as much to do with respecting personal space as with adopting a non-judgemental view of the story that accompanies the person. For many there is an implicit fear that joining the local church means being roped into things that they would rather not be involved in. For her, acceptance of her boundaries was important and acceptance of her daughter an implicit acceptance and empowering of her.

> I think that people are very welcoming to me. They have
> seen me before and I am someone who is around a bit. I
> find that nice. Also, things with Debbie, activities she has
> done have been great. People are good to her and that is
> nice for me. The initiative for me to come was her.   *(Sara,
> C3)*

Sara finds acceptance in the community that does not crowd her. She is able to remain in control of how she manages her life and yet still feel included. One feature of church community life is that, quite often the new*comer* doesn't feel fully accepted as a new *member*. Edna and Wally (C3) described their fear of this. Their subsequent experience of the welcome they received and the degree of acceptance they felt enables them to speak of St Luke's as an 'oasis'. Many people encounter Church in this way. The fear of rejection by established church members, perhaps for possessing uncertainties in areas of faith, implies a 'club' that wants to control its members rather than a community seeking to nurture them. As an elderly couple, Edna and Wally were prepared for the more senior and therefore established members of the congregation (as they perceived them) to resist befriending them. To their surprise they discovered this not to be the case.

> When we first come you think that all the regulars who have
> been there a hundred years, are they going to accept you?
> Funnily enough we got accepted easily enough. Everybody
> seems okay. I have heard of other churches where people
> don't get accepted.   *(Wally, C3)*

Sara and Wally have both discovered that common suppositions about church have not been borne out in their experience. The first is that when small congregations want to grow they look to the young rather than the elderly. Sara's incentive is her daughter, but she also finds something for herself. The second is that the elderly are the most conservative and therefore inflexible. Wally, himself a senior citizen, discovers the opposite to be true. In this instance St Luke's is described as a church in which the *status quo* is not a description of power held in the hands of the supposed traditional-ists (the senior/elderly members of the congregation). Nor is it one in which power is invested in the 'new youth' that a small church like St Luke's might otherwise be trying to cultivate.

New members seeking to ease their way into an established faith community might find the transition uncomfortable or even painful. What is likely is that they will perceive the inability to be inclusive as rejection of them personally. They will, in turn, reject the entire community and either look elsewhere or give up alto-gether. What church members seem to be describing in their reflections is not that there are no groups who exercise influence at their church, but that they (and consequently the influence) seems to be fairly well spread. If this is really so, then it is signifi-cant for the exercise of reflection on pastoral practice. The theology that comes from the base communities already described speaks of working 'from below to above'. It gives credibility to the insights and experiences of those at the baseline of the Church – everyday people. If this way of doing theological reflection with any local church community is to stand a chance of success it will probably have to take in a broad sample of members.

For Nathaniel of category C3 it was critical to his choice of a church community that this be the case. He had lived some distance from St Luke's church. His work brought him into the area and he came to the church on the recommendation of a friend who is a priest. St Luke's for him is a community of people who are racially, ethnically, socially and economically mixed. What was interesting was that he already knew that there would be an issue of power to deal with for a community with these social components, and the question of who holds power in such diverse communities is one that he now raises. Nathaniel could see that power was at work in the St Luke's community; what he liked was that it was not (as he saw it) in the hands of any one particular group. For him the litmus test was the way in which people were welcomed and who was welcomed.

The fact that there were mixed race couples there and there

were unmarried couples (not that I knew that right away), I could tell that this would not constitute a problem at St Luke's.   *(Nathaniel, C3)*

Leonardo Boff, a writer on liberation theology, suggests that we should move from a paradigm of a Church *for* the poor to a Church *of* and *with* the poor.[4] In doing this we need to raise the level of influence exercised by the laity. This is important if the sense of inclusion into the life of the Church is to be truly reclaimed by those who feel left out. In his assessment of St Luke's Nathaniel saw attempts at this reflected in the contributions lay people made to the life of worship in the church. His reflection records that he saw his church as a community that was interested in empowering its membership. He thought that this might be similarly reflected in the local church's ministry to the wider community.

> After a few Sundays it was quite obvious to me that there was a very mixed background and looking at those who participated in the service in an active way, those distributing communion and sidespeople, you could see was all very mixed. Charlton I found to be a very mixed neighbourhood. There are the urban priority areas and there is some very posh housing. It was very important to have all that and the fact that you could not pin point people. Some places you can see people in role. This was a place that seemed very empowering of the people.   *(Nathaniel, C3)*

Reflections on ethos and values within the local church

In drawing their picture of the local church, the members then tried to define the ethos of this community; its social, political and theological style, feel or flavour. How did they see themselves? What did they stand for?

Churchgoing people – an endangered species?
It would have been easy to expect an answer like 'Gay Rights'
or 'Blessing same-sex couples' when answering these questions.
Everyone knew the issue under examination in this book. However,
only two people mentioned it as a single issue, suggesting perhaps
that most church members see this issue as only one among many.
Furthermore none of the participants felt that they had become
members of St Luke's because of its stand over the issue of same-
sex partnerships. Generally speaking it was an integral part of a
whole ethos, consistent with and as unremarkable as the rest.

It was the young interviewees (C5) who made this the most
plain. Their church had 'atmosphere' and they saw it as a community struggling to develop a welcome for everybody. One
specified that he liked the very definite leaning towards those who
get left on the outside of things.

It was the young who first raised the topic of gay and lesbian
members of the congregation.

> St Luke's stands for young people. It has a youth focus
> service and tries to integrate adults and young people as
> well. Not all churches do that. It also tries to make gay and
> lesbian people feel welcome which is good.   *(Nicola, C5)*

What is particularly interesting is the way they did this. First, they
do not speak in abstract terms. There is no reference to homosexuality as a sexual condition, or homosexual acts, or stereotypical
groupings. They make no reference to 'gays' or 'lesbians' as if they
were a technical classification. Instead they adopt simple human
terms. These are gay and lesbian *people*, individuals with real lives,
not merely types. The second striking thing is their personal identification with gay and lesbian members of the congregation. What
they like about their church is that they feel it is as much theirs as
anyone's through the welcome they see in evidence. They say
clearly 'St Luke's stands for young people'. It is almost as if this is
the language of an endangered species. These churchgoing young
adults know from their school and other peer group experiences

that they are an unusual minority group because they attend church at all. Implicitly they know that the Church is in crisis. It is perceived as unattractive to most young people who respond by rejecting it.

The young people offer an implicit indication of the root of this unattractiveness. For them the kind of language that the Church deploys in its welcome is crucial. If it is a conditional welcome, it is most likely to meet rejection. When a church community attempts to welcome all, then it has to do just that. If the young have the experience of being marginalised in the wider Church and world they will identify with other groups in the same position. It is probably no coincidence that it is this group that first raise the identity of gay and lesbian people whom they may perceive as another 'minority group', perhaps similarly marginalised within the Church. In this instance their experience of a local Christian community has been one of acceptance for themselves. They count that as good.

> It stands for a community church. It welcomes all people.
> *(Alex, C5)*

From the ethnic minority category two members of the congregation described the ethos at St Luke's in a language of liberty.

> St Luke's stands for equal rights for everyone and I think it is a very good idea to include everyone in activities and everything that is going on in the church. *(Tina, C4)*

'Equal rights' is a phrase that is part of a civil culture and theological language that presupposes a wider vocabulary of oppression, liberation and injustice. It has been identified in the rise of feminist and Liberation theologies. It pays attention to and values the human experience. It is a phrase that has been accused of being inauthentic to the work of theology. John Stott, a respected Anglican evangelical theologian, is very wary of its use particularly in the wider debate about the inclusion of same-sex partners in the life of the Church.[5] Others, holding similar views, represent a mood apparent in some church communities that want to resist the influences of culture and context because they fear what they see as a sell-out of what they call 'traditional' Christian values. In their view, the contemporary Church in Western Europe and North America needs to make a stand against these encroaching secular influences within the Church.

This is in marked contrast to the African and Caribbean members of St Luke's who have found in it a specific 'equal rights' language with real meaning and significance. For them this is not the result of creeping secular influences but as a concept, a gift, born of their experiences as an ethnic group who have known both welcome and rejection. Instead it provides them with an adequate language to describe feelings and need. There is always a danger of mis-understanding when people are equipped with a new and dynamic language, as can be seen from the story at the beginning of this chapter. There the women discovered a way of expressing them-selves as women in a village community where they were not equal shareholders in the power of the community. Their way of seeing the resurrection narratives and what that revealed to them about women in their own culture became a threat to those who held sway in the community and they were silenced on two fronts; first by the men of the village who belittled their views, and then by the priest who used some academic theology to sustain the institutional Church line. It is from the ethnic minority category at St Luke's that we are offered the view that equal rights are not just for black and other ethnic minority groups, they are for *all*.

This theme of liberty was present in most of the interviewees and nearly everyone saw it as a value that made most sense to their church trying to work in the wider local community. If there was no appreciation of the freedom to value everyone, then their church had no real life or influence in that wider community. For Lavinia this was the best way to express a Gospel of love and social justice. She described this ethos as a catalyst to her personal liberation.

> St Luke's stands for the Gospel of Love. I think that sums
> it up. Love and social justice . . . I saw the church involved

in community. It fitted my view of the world, my socialist view of the world if you like. This was not a church that in my atheist days I saw as something that was repressive or authoritarian or high handed dogma. *(Lavinia, C1)*

What was freeing for Lavinia here was discovering that her local church held a religious ethos that she did not have to fit into. Instead, it fitted her. St Luke's thus begins to emerge as a community of faith that can allow individuals the opportunity to find liberty and have their lives transformed.

Having described the ethos of their community life as one which stands for liberty and equal rights, the church members go on to provide illustrations of inclusiveness and involvement. Mary (C2) recalled occasions when her church made a stand for the individual and for minority groups.

I think that it has always been important that St Luke's has stood for the individual as an individual, and therefore it has always supported you might say, minority groups, if in other situations these groups were less well supported. I am thinking particularly of the ministry of women in the wider sense and I would also add the acceptance of different people's sexuality. *(Mary, C2)*

What we have here is a description of how being different is a positive thing. For Mary, an ethos that is open and non-judgemental might enable a theology of difference to emerge which reveals every individual as made in the image of God while challenging the capacity of her church community to be fully accepting. Being counted in is itself a liberating experience.

I would always want to be part of a church that had an attitude that valued individuals, didn't make judgements and accepted everybody in their own relationship with God. *(Mary, C2)*

Mary reminds us that part of the ethos of a church community is that it attempts to cultivate a relationship with God. St Luke's is a faith community, but it is another church member, in the intermediate category this time, who highlighted this.

Sally described faith sharing as the fundamental feature that drew her to the life of not only the church community but the parish community as well. Not only does St Luke's embrace diversity of opinion, but, as she sees it, it can hold unusual individuals within its community.

> . . . God doesn't really have a lot of breathing spaces in many places but I wouldn't say that of St Luke's. I think that God has breathing space there. *(Sally, C2)*

What she describes as the breath of God is what makes this particular church community vibrant for her.

Those who were newest to St Luke's corroborated the description of local church ethos made by those who have been part of it for a few or many years. Sara contrasted it with the austerity of the Roman Catholic Church she had grown up in. She and Daisy appreciated the openness and flexibility of the preaching and teaching ministry. In it they found all the diversity of the local community. Roger admired the efforts to see ministry carried into the local community. Wally and Edna were glad of its continuity with the past and Nathaniel saw it as a place where he could be truly himself in expressing his views and opinions. He actually moved house so that he could live in the parish and be nearer the church.

Reflecting on recovering the Rodney and Saxon story

By looking at what they have found attractive about being at St Luke's the participants have been able to describe characteristics of their community that we have marked as the 'ethos' of the church. In effect what they have done is to set the context for their attempt at recovering an important part of St Luke's story. It is the story of the arrival at St Luke's of the first *openly* gay couple and the effect of events surrounding this arrival.

A brief background outline

In 1978 Tony Crowe, the then rector of St Luke's, featured in a local newspaper article with the headline 'Gay love is okay says rebel vicar'. A man called Saxon Lucas subsequently telephoned him. Saxon asked Tony if he would be prepared to bless a same-gender union he and his partner had been in for 19 years. The rector agreed. The ceremony took place at St Luke's in November 1978. In early 1979 the couple moved into the parish and became worshipping members of the church. Eight months after their ceremony of blessing took place, the event was reported in the local and national press:

Gay couple 'married' by vicar Tony

A vicar has opened the doors of his church to homosexuals who want to marry. The Rev Tony Crowe has come out in support of gay couples, and has already 'married' two men who have lived together for nineteen years.[6]

Uproar over gay 'wedding' service

A storm has broken over a vicar's confession that he 'married' a homosexual couple. A bishop admitted this week that he knew nothing of the ceremony. And some church members have called for the sacking of the Rev Tony Crowe, who admitted conducting a special blessing for two gays who had lived together for 19 years.[7]

Rodney and Saxon remained committed members of St Luke's congregation until they left London in 1986 to open a restaurant in the West Country. By 1999, both had died.

As members of the church began to think about and reflect on this story, what it meant to them and how it had influenced their current attitudes, James Hopewell's theory of individuals joining church communities where the community story finds common characteristics with their own life story emerges. In every category, church members had either known Rodney and Saxon personally or had heard of them.

As they speak about this story from the church community's past the members begin to describe Rodney and Saxon in terms that they have already used to describe the ethos of St Luke's and their attraction to it. In particular the senior and intermediate members reveal striking similarities in their reflections on Rodney and Saxon. Almost without exception there is a genuine sense of affection for them as individuals and as a couple. The intimacy of this community of friends reveals itself in the way they talk about the friendship inspired by the couple. First, it is clear that this is a church community that meets not only when it is time for worship. Second, Rodney and Saxon are described as a couple who allowed church life to spill over into the hospitality of their home life.

As a couple Rodney and Saxon gained a reputation for entertaining at home and established a ministry of hospitality and welcome. Hospitality and welcome have been principal themes describing the ethos of church life at St Luke's. Numerous interviewees described the church as a place in which they felt welcomed and at home. Jennifer (C1) was at pains to declare that in her friendship with them she simply saw them as two likeable men. Most others were the same in their assessment. They are described by some as artistic or theatrical, one of them quite voluble, the other taciturn, as 'pillars of the church', as hospitable, helpful and generous. Most simply thought them good company.

One person recalled the day of the blessing ceremony.

> My first memory was the way the church was decorated with the flowers when they came for their blessing. I used to do the flowers then and they said to me 'Wait until you see the church on Sunday.' There was this highly over-decorated church, which was staggering. What I remember about them was that they were very helpful in doing things. They were very generous. I liked them. *(Jennifer, C1)*

This is an important detail. Jennifer mentioned nothing of the service itself but commended and upheld Rodney and Saxon's faithfulness. She went on to say that it was, in her view, the blessing of a relationship of 20 years' standing which, had it been between a man and woman, no one would have opposed. She conveyed a story in which the characters are their actions. They are generous and effusive. They draw attention and some admiration. They pose questions without demanding answers and they provoke serious thought and discussion in their request for a church blessing.

What Jennifer manages to convey here is that Rodney and Saxon are a wider story, personified. Elsewhere in the Church a debate relating to homosexual acts/practices and so on was going on. Here at St Luke's in 1979 the same story, with the same issues, was given two human faces, friends within the company of friends.

Some other interviewees besides Jennifer recognised the significance of this experience within the broader context of the then national Church-wide debate. The experience of knowing Saxon and Rodney, far from polarising the discussion surrounding the issues concerning same-sex attraction, instead gave it another dimension. This was not a debate in the abstract about homosexuality. It was a living concern that focused on the lives of two individuals who were, for most of the church community, friends. Mary (C2) described how Rodney and Saxon became her friends before she ever considered the issue of their sexual orientation.

> We arrived at St Luke's at a time when the homosexuality issue was coming to the fore. I think it was after the time that their union was blessed. We came to know them as individuals. They became friends, good friends and not simply members of the congregation we were part of. We had not been properly faced with this as a question I suppose if I am honest.   (Mary, C2)

This experience propelled Mary and her husband into addressing the underlying issues because it was centred on real people whom they already knew and liked. Saxon and Rodney afforded Mary and the whole congregation at St Luke's an experience that was marked not just in the enactment of one ceremony but in the week by week living alongside a committed gay couple. Getting to know Saxon and Rodney as they would get to know any other couple who had committed their lives in such a way *was* a different kind of experience. Until Mary met them she admits that this was not a question she had properly faced, but the Christian commitment of the couple in question was not in doubt, they were key figures in the life of the local church, 'pillars of the church' and men who individually demonstrated the warmth and generous hospitality that are marks of the Christian Gospel.

Interestingly, the service of blessing for Saxon and Rodney in 1979 coincided and was compared with the high level of importance attached to women's ministry at that time, women's ordained ministry in particular. One member was uncertain as to whether the two might be related issues and speculated that one would be perceived as a 'moral' issue and the other not. I am not so sure. The two issues are certainly related. The injustice of the women's issue that concerned the local church at that time was indeed a moral issue. It was concerned with social change and how that might be facilitated. It was concerned with sexual equality. It was concerned with honouring sexual identity and how the whole Church might keep faith with all those who wanted to test their vocations to the priesthood. It raised issues of how women might be visible in the Church and why some did not want them to be. These issues concerning social change, truthful sexual identity, faithfulness and openness were all issues raised again in this story of Rodney and Saxon.

Faithfulness and commitment were what nearly everyone wanted to endorse in Rodney and Saxon. So if this is a moral story it is recognised as such by those interviewed, and one that affects every level of the church. Support for Rodney and Saxon was deemed justifiable on several fronts. It was not only thought to be right in itself, it was also felt to be deeply Christian.

The Rodney and Saxon story was important but could never be read in isolation. The service of covenant, blessing and commitment that took place in 1978 and the service of celebration for their 25 years in partnership in 1985 were markers in the history of our church. But, more important, these events and the time spent in between bound together not only the two men who loved each other, but also the community of faith that they had become part of and which had become part of them. By attending the ceremony and recounting the event 20 years on Mary re-lives her own testimony that

> At the end of the day you decide where you stand and that is part of being a Christian. If that is what you believe then that is what you stand for and what comes as a result is just life. *(Mary, C2)*

For most of those who could remember them, the sexual orientation of the two men was irrelevant. What was important was knowing them and liking them as friends. Only two interviewees made any reference to their sexual orientation. For Lavinia Rodney and Saxon's sexual orientation was never a thing to be 'discovered'. They appeared as a couple and were as open about that as any other couple might be. In St Luke's they seemed to see a community that could sustain them and hold them in what most churches would regard as an unusual lifestyle.

Arthur is the other church member who makes any reference to their sexual orientation. It is his starting point in describing them.

> What I know about those two is that they are or were homosexuals. *(Arthur, C2)*

Arthur declared that he had no personal animosity towards either gay man. He is even prepared to concede that after the fuss of the press coverage surrounding their service of blessing had died down and they themselves had settled into the community:

> They seemed, generally, to be liked and the vast majority didn't mind them.

The ethnic minority category (C4) had few memories between them, although some were aware of the story in its 'legendary' status. The youth category (C5) were all aware of the Rodney and Saxon story, as a church story, though few could name any details. One teenager knew that they were his godparents and he knew they were a couple but that had not been a problem for him.

What remains of the Rodney Madden and Saxon Lucas story in the day-to-day life of St Luke's can be seen first as a commitment to support same-gender couples who come seeking the ministry of the church, and second as an ethos that will have been embellished by the experience begun in 1978 and which continues to the present day. What impact this has upon current thinking and practice within the church will be seen later. The effect and influence of the story on the church community will be considered in the voices of the couples who make their way to St Luke's. We will look at these in the next chapter.

CHAPTER 4

Voices in Partnership

listening to the couples

> Heard melodies are sweet but those unheard are sweeter.[1]

In Chapter Three the reader was introduced to a sample of the congregation at St Luke's. I outlined how members of the congregation came to be at the local parish church and why they have continued to stay. In the following chapters I will return to those members in an attempt to reflect upon and give some analysis to the pastoral practice of blessing the unions of same-gender partners as experienced in the 20 years since that shared between Rodney and Saxon. One purpose of this exercise was to allow voices not usually heard in this controversial discussion within the Church to speak. Chapter Three allowed those voices to begin their testimonies. In this chapter I now turn my attention to another group of hidden voices that are a necessary part of the discussion, namely the couples themselves.

What the members of the congregation at St Luke's have in common is that, as was the case for Saxon and Rodney, many of them have had the experience of being welcomed as strangers by the local church. What has happened as a result of this welcome is that they have moved from a place on the edge into the heart of the worshipping community. For many this move to the centre where they became more involved and committed to the local church community life came about as the result of an initial pastoral encounter in which they were served. It has always seemed to me that one of the great strengths of the Church was its ability to exist to serve those outside it in the first instance. Those of us who have been in pastoral practice for some time know that not all those we encounter on the edges move to the centre and become church members. Most do not. However what is critical for the Church in its mission and ministry is that it continues to make space for such encounters.

There are many people who encounter the Church in moments of pastoral crisis and who have no wish to enter the centre of the church community, but either move on, glad of what was offered, or maintain low levels of contact. There are countless examples of people met in this way either through a baptism, funeral or wedding ceremony. It seems to be an important reason for the Church's very existence.

Of the couples who shared their insights about each other and what they thought they were doing and their view of the Church, none have become members of St Luke's in the way Rodney and Saxon did. However, all have maintained some kind of contact. Some return for special events. Two couples made a point of returning on the anniversary of blessing. One couple asked for a renewal of vows on the anniversary of their commitment ceremony. This is much the same kind of request as that of married hetero-sexual couples who celebrate anniversaries by returning to the place where they first took their vows, and celebrating a renewal. In requesting marriage in church they may never have intended to become members of the local church but feel that they can approach the church to receive its ministry. In January 2000, one partner in one of the couples died. St Luke's was the only safe place that felt familiar and with a sufficient sense of home about it that his partner could turn to for the funeral service.

Listening to the couples

In their conference resolution of 1998 the bishops of the Anglican Communion pledged themselves to listen to the experiences of homosexual people.[2] What follows here will, I hope, offer some insights into the experiences of some same-gender couples. Each couple has approached St Luke's church to seek the pastoral support and care the individuals feel they need in making a commitment to another person of the same sex and to ask for blessing upon that union. The insights are based upon interviews with a sample of six couples who have had services of blessing for their unions over a period of six years. Some names have been changed.

The couples

Couple 1. Christina and Daniela

Christina is a 61-year-old Italian woman living in south-east London. She has been resident in the United Kingdom for more than 40 years having been married to an Englishman and widowed. She has three children from that marriage. She is particularly close to her daughter who has full knowledge of her relationship with Daniela and is supportive of them both. Daniela is 53 years old. She too is Italian and is a senior lecturer in modern languages at a university in Italy. Christina and Daniela have known each other for over 20 years. They had a service of covenanted union a year before being interviewed for this research.

Couple 2. Amelia and Ruth

Amelia is 34 years old. She grew up in Nottingham where she lived for 19 years with her parents in a middle-class home. She has a university education and is a qualified nurse. She is the mother of their 18-month-old daughter conceived through artificial insemination at a London clinic. Ruth is 33 years old. She was born and raised in Guernsey and is the fourth of five children to a mother and stepfather. She joined the army at 17 and served for eight years before leaving to join the Metropolitan Police. She has been employed in the police service for seven years. Amelia and Ruth are homeowners and live in south-east London. They had a service of covenanted union three years before being interviewed.

Couple 3. Karen and Anna

Karen is a 27-year-old woman born in London who has been married and divorced, and has two children. She was educated at a local south London state school. She is a care assistant, and self-employed hairdresser when between jobs. Anna is a 26-year-old Yorkshire woman educated at grammar school before training at catering college. They live in a council flat in a neighbouring parish and had a service of covenanted union three months prior to being interviewed.

Couple 4. Chris and Paul

Paul is a 32-year-old accountant working in London. He describes himself as the younger of two children in a happy family and home life. Chris is 39 years old. Born in London he has lived locally all his life. He has two older sisters and describes home life and upbringing as not very happy. He had a state school education to 'O' level standard and he now works for social services. Paul and Chris own their own home in south-east London a few miles from St Luke's parish. It is 18 months since they had their service of covenanted union.

Couple 5. Steve and Ian

Ian is 43 years old and grew up within a working-class household. He has two sisters, and both parents are elderly. He works for the legal aid board and likes to paint. Steve is 37 years old and works for the local healthcare trust in the casualty department. He too comes from what he describes as a working-class background. His father died when he was 19 and his mother married again. He has two brothers and a stepsister; both brothers are married and one has three children. Steve is currently training for a diploma in counselling. Steve and Ian have recently bought an apartment flat in a new development about five miles from St Luke's. Two months have passed since they took part in a service of covenanted union.

Couple 6. Stephen and Douglas

Stephen is 39 years old. He was born and raised in the east end of London. Brought up in a middle-class home and educated in the state school system he described a fear of sitting exams. He secured a good job with a drug and chemical company though now he is not working due to poor health. Douglas is 33 years old, and was brought up in Surrey, where he attended an Independent school as a boarder. He has pursued no career as such and spends most of his time caring for Stephen. Both men are HIV positive and renew their vows of blessing every year. They were interviewed six years after their service of covenanted union.

With the exception of Christina and Daniela whose ethnicity might be described as Latin/Mediterranean, all couples might be classified as white Anglo-Saxon.

Knowing me, knowing you

All relationships have a beginning and couples often describe that beginning as a moment of 'finding' each other. At this point we look at that moment of 'finding'. This will contrast with what couples and church members discovered in 'finding' a church that met their needs and could help them. But relationships are not only about beginnings and the chapter continues by exploring with the couples two major areas of interest. The first of these is about what they have identified as important in their friendship with each other, the second about the ways they viewed the Church before they found a local church to celebrate their partnership with. It looks a little at expectations and will seek to establish whether there is any link between models of the Church that might emerge and what they have found in each other in their relationships. All of those interviewed had some experience of a church encounter. Often these were minimal and located only in the past. Sometimes the renewal of contact with a priest and a church community as they prepared for their service of blessing was one in which sparks of faith came alive in them. Two couples had been raised as Catholics with quite varying experiences, and

75

this coloured their decision to explore their journey of love and friendship with a partner of the same sex in the institutional Church.

Making an approach to the local church when you have spent much of your life outside it can be a daunting task. It was an experience that quite a number of church members could relate to. Crossing the threshold for the first time was not something that many did with ease. Some church members described feeling anxious about only finding their way to the church when their lives were in particular need. One person had been dogged with ill health and had renewed her acquaintance with her local church on more than one occasion. Others found they made their way to church for other reasons. One came to escort an elderly parent, another because kindness was shown by the clergy in a moment of distress. However, for both couples and church members, whether in their personal relationships or in seeking meaning and purpose to their lives as Christians, it was a sense of belonging that they sought. Furthermore the desire to see secure relationships built was important to both church members and couples alike. Each considered it significant for building a healthy society and a strong sense of community. Many had come from the edge to the centre of the church community because of a desire to build that into their lives. Some described a bereavement either through death or the breakdown of a relationship, through which they found acceptance in a new community. Others had found that acceptance borne out in the cultivation of new and lasting friendships.

Servant and friend

Friendship as a way of being in relationship seems to have come under review particularly in the wake of an upsurge of theological writing on sexuality and gender issues. What does it mean to be 'good friends'? Is it no more than a benign description of a vague way of relating that no other title will more accurately describe? How do Christians understand the relational change between Jesus and the apostles as accorded in the fourth gospel when he describes them as no longer servants but friends?[3] The writer of the fourth gospel characterises this friendship as one marked by a kind of intimacy. It is an intimacy through which he describes to the reader the things that God has revealed to Jesus. In other words, what marks the disciples' translation from servants to friends are the insights that Jesus has been entrusted with by God and is then prepared to share with them, his closest followers.

What we might deduce from this particular image of friendship is that it is accorded an elevated status. To be 'friend' is a superior way of relating. It carries with it the respect and confidence of knowing and understanding that this is the supreme model of human relationship. It is perhaps important to recover this insight since the status that many accord friendship in our age is not quite the same. Sometimes friendship is mistaken for a hearty, back-slapping, drinking companion styled relationship which never elevates itself beyond the superficial. At other times it is a term that is utilised in such a way as to lend suspicion to the relationship. It is a 'polite front' for a relationship that might be more than it would seem. Thus, the use of the term 'friends' in some circles is confused or mistrusted.

I was particularly struck by what I perceived to be a 'suspicion' of friendship at a meeting I attended for incumbent clergy who were to receive new training clergy. As part of the training pro-gramme we spent some time with a (female) incumbent and her (female) new curate who had been working together for the last year. As they described their time together it all seemed very rosy. They never seemed to disagree and there was clear mutual respect. At the end of the session I asked them how they dealt with their differences. It was clearly a difficult question to answer and amongst the things that they described was a relationship of friend-ship. 'We're really good friends,' they said. I remember feeling the excitement of one about to unearth a new discovery. Perhaps we were about to witness a significant practical theology of non-competitive relationships and how women in ordained ministry had a new model that all of us could benefit from. However, that discussion didn't happen. When pressed for some definition of what it meant to be 'really good friends' nothing of the sort emerged. Friendship was merely a way of socialising.

My sadness in recounting the above experience lies not in the thought that the vicar and her curate didn't socialise together, but rather that it gave a colourful illustration of how I think friendship is often perceived. It is because friendship has for so many been no more than a description of their relationship with those with whom they socialise that we are left with an insubstantial concept. Those who shared in the preparation of this book challenge that view. What the church community at St Luke's articulates in Chapter Two is endorsed at the beginning of this chapter by the gay and lesbian couples who make their way to the church for support and acceptance and a service of blessing. Friendship is an important component in relationships of intimacy. For communities and couples alike there needs to be a recovery of friendship in relationships.

The recovery of friendship

> Friendships arise out of particular needs and circumstances; they spring from particular desires and commitments of individuals in community. They are generosities born of special limitations.[4]

Many of those engaged in scholarly research have spent time looking at the nature of friendship and its significance in theology for our ongoing understanding of God. For some of them the recovery of friendship as a significant constituent in intimate relationships has been a notable feature of their research and writing. So, for some, like Mary Hunt, an exploration of a feminist view of friendship in relationships of significance, leads her to argue that what women lovers look for in their relationships is intimacy and not what she calls 'genitality'.[5] If friendship can be seen as a place of intimacy rather than merely a social forum for particular individuals or a polite front for a physical relationship, then this view breaks new ground in our understanding of intimacy and friendship. Other scholars like Adrian Thatcher tell us that it is insights like this that allow us to break the mould of friendship as we have known it. This is important because ultimately Christians see the disclosure of God's love in human friendship. However, Thatcher goes on to describe a view of friendship that has been handed on to us by men. He begins with the writing of Aristotle who gave a good deal of attention to human friendship, but reminds us that Aristotle drew examples only from educated young males. Women were described as defective, and along with the elderly and inferior classes, were deemed as incapable of friendships based on virtue. This classical inheritance was passed to the early Christian churches and influenced in particular the development of monastic communities under the spread of Roman Catholicism. Friendships amongst men in community life were non-sexual because it was perceived to be a higher and more virtuous way of living. If these structures are removed, says Thatcher, we are left with the challenging question of why all friendships outside marriage should retain compulsory celibacy. The new insights of women scholars, he tells us, challenge exactly what constitutes the most important components of intimacy and friendship.[6]

Some of those women scholars themselves argue for the need to dismantle the inherited way of thinking about intimacy and friendship because it has left us with a one-sided and thus impaired view of friendship. Mary Hunt argues that this needs to be transformed for perhaps three good reasons. First, a male only view of friendship has had a serious impact on the friendships of women. Second, those who define what is authentic about and acceptable to human friendship, hold the reins of power in cultures and societies. Third, those who hold the power define the context in which we live. Because we have received a one-sided understanding of intimacy and friendship in Western Europe and North America, we have also received an expectation that we are to be heterosexual in our lives and loves.[7] If we really are to see friendship as the disclosure of God's love, then not only is it important to retrieve a fuller picture of friendships between women and men, but also serious attention must be given to the understanding of intimacy and friendship as expressed between partners of the same sex.

For these reasons, some time was spent with couples who had prepared for a service of covenanted union at St Luke's. Each was asked to reflect and comment on the elements of the relationship which were most valued. What was revealed in their answers was almost universal gratitude for the place of friendship within a relationship of faithful commitment. Amongst the women two couples had formed friendships that had sustained them long before they had entered a partnership of commitment. The women speak in terms of these friendships being important for support of each other. It was an important prelude to a relationship of intimacy and corroborates the theory that Hunt espouses. For some there was no certainty that living a life of commitment to each other was the thing to do from the outset. Rather, it would seem that the stability of their growing friendship was something that enabled them to grow in an understanding of what they finally wanted their relationship to be.

> We really started as friends, just really good friends, which actually feels quite significant and did then as well. We were a great support for each other. *(Amelia, Couple 2)*

> It felt like the first 18 months when we had been friends was a vetting, which was strange because neither of us had actively decided about this relationship. There was no pressure from either side. *(Ruth, Couple 2)*

> More of the emphasis was about could we share our lives together? Could we actually live on a day-to-day basis. The emphasis was quite practical really. The love came later. *(Amelia)*

The men all seem to have met at convened social events. Paul placed an ad in the Hitching Post of the *Farmers' Weekly* and met Chris on a blind date. Their relationship bonded quite quickly but what they found in it was a place of safety. It was a way of being together that they could trust.

> I think it was quite clear from the beginning that we were quite comfortable with each other. We could be quite open with each other, which is why I think things went so well.
> (*Chris, Couple 4*)

Steve and Ian met in a pub but declare that now that they have found each other they tend to avoid the pub and club scene, and prefer instead to remain at home. Stephen and Douglas met in a nightclub and almost moved in with each other straight away. What is particularly interesting is not so much the relative speed at which these relationships move from meeting to living together but what drives that. Each couple describes a realisation that they are searching for life security in a faithful partnership. This is a far cry from the stereotype that all gay partnerships are fleeting, shallow and promiscuous. Here are people looking for stability, affection and friendship.

> I think that we have grown very close. I think about Ian when I am not with him and he is just a really most marvellous person. I think that we have our ups and downs like most couples, nothing is a bed of roses, but I feel we are able to talk through things and we never leave each other without apologising or making up. (*Steve, Couple 5*)

> I have been very grateful for that and it is something that has brought us together even more really. Any crisis I have had has been held by the relationship really. So our relationship has blossomed and developed. (*Ian, Couple 5*)

The search for a church: seeking a place of hospitality, sanctuary and empowerment

In Chapter Three we saw members of the church community reflect on what they felt it meant to be 'Church'. What brought each of the church members into the life of St Luke's they described in three models of Church. The first of these described the local church as a community of hospitality, the second a place of safety or sanctuary and the third a community of empowerment. What we now see is that couples, having reflected upon what brought them together and what they valued in each other, begin to think about why they approached the local church to affirm their partnership. Not unusually, many of the values they were looking for in the Church each had already found in their relationship with the other.

Like most other strands of society, it would appear that gay and lesbian culture is a pluralistic culture. There is a perceived 'counter culture' in large parts of the gay and lesbian community which does not see the need to adopt the relational models of opposite-sex couples in a predominantly heterosexual world view of things.

> The situation for homosexual couples is the opposite of heterosexual marriage: gays are stigmatised for coupling, rewarded for uncoupling. Furthermore, in the gay community, endings are not seen as tragic, nor are they negatively sanctioned.[8]

If this is so, then those couples who have made their way to St Luke's know that they are within a minority in this pluralistic culture. Some will be supported by their friends but perceived by others as caving in to a social convention that has perpetuated the predominating view that opposite-sex relations in an ideal lifelong partnership are not only the norm but the only framework for living as a couple. Thus, couples seeking the support of the Church are already vulnerable, rejected by others within the gay and lesbian community because of their search for acceptance within the Church. But having made this decision to seek acceptance in the Church they also know that they run the risk of rejection here too. By and large the Church is perceived to be a conservative and traditional institution. So why bother with such a risky journey? For Saxon and Rodney it was an easier question to answer. They were already located within the worshipping community. This is not so for the others.

Christina and Daniela begin by struggling even to articulate their reasons for finding a church. At first it does not match their stereotype of what the Church exists for. Theirs has been a Mediterranean Catholic upbringing with a perspective of Christian life that does not allow them to reconcile what they have been taught about the Christian way and the feelings that they have felt growing for each other for over 20 years. They do not expect to find acknowledgement from the Church they were formed and nurtured in.

> I had not thought about it. My idea before was that it was not a normal relationship. If it was not normal then why enter the normal path? If it is different then it has got to be different, but then she had this idea and my own idea began to change.   *(Daniela, Couple 1)*

But in the struggle to find a language that conveys the meaning, they implicitly communicate a deep feeling of wanting to be taken seriously and knowing of no other social institution that could, if it would, meet them at such a deep level. Sharing these feelings openly cannot, for them, take place in *any* venue. Ironically, the place where they most want to feel safe, publicly, is the very Church they feel sure will reject them.

> Because . . . I don't know . . . we started the relations and it was good and I think for me it was how I feel and I realise that she was the only one that was in my heart. I never have any women person in my life before but with her it was different.   *(Christina, Couple 1)*

The search to be taken seriously was shared by most couples. Many expressed frustration in that search and a sense of being treated unequally in a system that generously serves marriage couples who have no more commitment to Christian worship than they.

We didn't want a spectacle or a circus because there is a lot of people out there doing those things and it is not us. We didn't want that. What we wanted was to have a commitment ceremony for us, for our friends so that our friends could share in celebration of our relationship. And that we could do that and have our relationship blessed in church and have God involved. It was important that we could do that in a church as anyone else could. *(Ruth, Couple 2)*

Yes there was a societal thing as well. Part of the decision was about wanting to be able to approach the Church the same as anyone else. *(Amelia, Couple 2)*

Others endorsed this view, emphasising their knowledge of what was already available to them but offering a new perspective. Churches are public places of a different kind to pubs, clubs or other venues where same-gender couples might be able to secure a liturgy or ceremony of affirmation and blessing. They are genuine public places in that they cannot be 'hired' for an event, but remain open. As with any act of public worship, anyone can join the proceedings whether invited or not. All couples expressed their wish for openness in which their own sense of serious participation and intent could be seen.

To me the Church is a place where if a gay couple can get recognised then it seems more acceptable than a blessing in a pub or on a street corner. No, what is really important is to make the vows. *(Anna, Couple 3)*

It means more for gay weddings to be held in churches that in pubs. I've been to a gay wedding in a pub. It's not the same. *(Karen, Couple 3)*

Ian didn't feel too comfortable with the idea of a 'mock' wedding . . . that wasn't for me and I didn't think it was for Ian as well. Ian asked me last year to get blessed and I was

> really touched. Ian had asked me to do something that I
> knew he wanted to do as well. He wasn't doing it just to
> make me happy, he really wanted to get involved in some-
> thing. I thought right we have got to take this seriously and
> the most appropriate way to do this would be to have a
> church blessing. *(Steve, Couple 5)*

> We've never really termed it a substitute for marriage but
> we thought that the idea of a covenant was really important
> and gradually the religious side of it has come to mean more
> as well. *(Ian, Couple 5)*

None of the couples were currently members of a faith community, but all were mindful that what they sought and where it
took place must reflect the serious nature of how they felt for each
other and how that was to be reflected in a serious setting. All but
two of those questioned had some previous faith-forming connection with the institutional Church. This was usually an experience
of childhood and early adolescence. However for Ruth, as we have
seen, it provided a platform that allowed her to access a language
of faith as she articulated her desire for blessing: this was a ceremony that was to 'have God involved'. Of the others, it was
Stephen (Couple 6) who most explicitly expressed the act of covenanted union as one that he made to his partner as if he were in
the presence of God. For him, the Church as a place of hospitality
and welcome was somewhere in which he found reassurance and
strength for his partnership with Douglas. This he still finds, particularly when (like all relationships – married or otherwise) that
partnership endures times of stress.

> When it came down to it and the time came when we chose
> to go to church I think that we just needed some reassurance
> that we were really committed and by exchanging rings in
> front of witnesses and Our Lord has made it that much
> more special. Somehow that has lingered on in a way that
> is difficult to explain, but if I get really upset and angry, I'll
> say to Doug, 'Look, if it is going to be like this, should we

split up?' He says to me, 'So, does that mean that the blessing meant nothing?' and it all comes back to me. It is that part. I told God that we are always going to be together and I am not going to break my promise to the Lord.
(Stephen, Couple 6)

Stephen's confidence in the Church was not one that was readily shared by all couples. Some had found that their past experience of Church had not been warm, others had simply 'outgrown' what the Church seemed to offer. The couples revealed their current understanding of Church to be based either upon limited encounters at a personal level or through general perceptions gained via the media. All couples were aware that parts of the Church were hostile to same-gender couples.

It was not something that I had considered and thought it was something that the Church wouldn't accept. *(Chris, Couple 4)*

Same-gender couples seeking the blessing of the Church are placed in an awkward position compared to opposite-gender couples seeking marriage. Their principal perception of the Church they hope to be served by is one that needs careful searching to find genuine welcome and hospitality. Most of those finding their way to St Luke's do so through referral from Gay Switchboard, or the Lesbian and Gay Christian Movement or by word of mouth. Steve and Doug had attended a friend's service of blessing. Ruth and Amelia, unusually, had come across St Luke's indirectly, via the Rodney and Saxon story as it had been spilled in sections of the press. Despite describing the story as 'not very complimentary' it made connections for them. Just as many of the congregation had made their way to the church community because the 'church story' had connected with their 'personal, life story', so Amelia and Ruth, after much careful researching, decided to take the plunge. It seemed to them to be a place that would meet them where they were rather than judging them and telling them where they ought to be.

I had no real formal contact with the Church, just now and again with weddings and christenings and whatever. I've always believed that you don't have to go to church to be a believer, but I thought that it was the right place to go to. Yes, I was nervous that we were going to be rejected, so I was really pleased when we weren't. *(Paul, Couple 4)*

Fear of, and actual rejection can be a devastating experience and one that causes incalculable damage to any future pastoral relationship. Yet it is something that happens too often at every level of church life.

About six years ago I looked again at the Church and I wanted to find out more. I went to a local church, to their 'Just Looking' group. I attended about eight meetings and was quite disappointed by the way I was accepted by the church. Once they found out I was gay I was certainly not made to feel as welcome and I was more or less told that if I was in a gay relationship that I wouldn't go to heaven and I was dissuaded from being in a relationship. *(Chris, Couple 4)*

Chris and Paul found St Luke's church a place of sanctuary. It was a safe place in which they did not have to justify who they were or apologise for their lifestyle. Chris remarked how traditional the worship had been when they attended on Sundays as part of their preparation. It stood in marked contrast to the very modern church he had tried to attend through the 'Just Looking' group. His first impression had been that modern externals might have represented a new and generous way of thinking, but instead he found himself judged and patronised. It was within the relative formality of an ancient church building with a wide cross-section of different people that he discovered a place of hospitality and sanctuary.

One person found himself on a new journey following this encounter. Ian had previously had no formal Christian faith but through the process of preparing for a service of covenanted union and blessing, felt the seeds of faith germinating within. It was something that had taken him completely by surprise.

> I was under the impression that it (the service of blessing) was on much more of a private scale. We would just come along and see you and you would say Come into church and we will do this in front of the altar or something like that. I thought it would be a blessing with that kind of context. Then we got more involved with the preparation and I was fine about that. I actually thought it was a very good idea . . . my background has never been particularly religious though my parents brought us up as Christians and they always had a certain respect for the Church. It has only been more recently, in the last few months that I have felt more spiritual.   *(Ian, Couple 5)*

What kind of Church is it anyway?

Those of us who co-exist within the institutional Church are often surprised at how we are perceived by those who live on the edge and wonder whether a move to the centre is one that they want to make. National press coverage is often the only picture they see. Much of the time the national Church is depicted as an irrelevant figure of fun. Statistics of falling numbers of churchgoing Christians are held as ample proof that we have entered a post-Christian era and that it is simply a matter of time before the sleepy giant dies of neglect. The couples were asked to give an overview of what they perceived the Church of England to be and why they had made an approach to a local church that was part of it.

Almost without exception the couples expressed gratitude for a Church of diversity and difference. While that difference was usually benchmarked by the experience of their own Church denomination (where it was different), there was also a general appreciation that somewhere within the diversity there would be a place for them in receiving its ministry. Most were clear that there would not be universal acceptance within any single denomination, let alone the Church of England, but there seemed to be sufficient attraction in the 'sleepy giant' to want to try.

Some were clear that their advance into the Church of England was made because they would have been rejected in their own Church.

> I didn't know anything much about the position of the Church of England, but I just guessed that it wouldn't be as problematic as that of the Catholic Church. That was just against. *(Daniela, Couple 1)*

> I found the Church of England a lot different to the Roman Catholic Church. I know for a fact that the Roman Catholic Church would not have helped us in the same way. *(Karen, Couple 3)*

> We were quite careful about who we approached in the Church because I think that of all the organisations and people that we dealt with the Church was the most frightening. We are both Catholic and knew that we couldn't contact the Catholic Church, and so we didn't. *(Ruth, Couple 2)*

> We thought there would at least be the potential for somebody in the Church of England to be accepting of us. *(Amelia, Couple 2)*

Others were uncertain of finding acceptance in any part of the Church of England.

> I wasn't sure if the Church of England would have anything to do with us because of the things you read and hear about. Also, my mum is a born-again Christian and she said that the Church wouldn't accept us. *(Anna, Couple 3)*

> Well, it's like with the media and people's views of it. They

always seem to be very archaic saying that we wouldn't be accepted.   *(Paul, Couple 4)*

Amelia and Ruth had taken a lot of trouble to find not only a place that would accept them but also a place where their faith values would be met. Simply to be 'gay friendly' was not enough. Others had described their reluctance for a secular ceremony in a pub, club or tent on the Gay Pride march. They had investigated the Metropolitan church, found it very affable, but not for them in this instance.

> We were put in touch with a few people like the Metropolitan church and we weren't comfortable with it. It wasn't right for *us*.   *(Ruth, Couple 2)*

> We looked at their stuff and thought that we just didn't fit into that way of thinking even though they share some similar Christian values. We don't believe that there is not a God which they are very clear about.   *(Amelia, Couple 2)*

Ian, who had found that preparing for a service of covenanted union had moved him to reflect quite deeply on what he described as the 'spiritual' side of things, found that the Church connected with his own sense of political justice. For him the welcoming, safe Church was one that had the capacity to stand on the side of the 'poor'. He had seen the Church that he found himself approaching as one that prized liberty as an important life value.

> Back in the 1980s I was quite impressed with the Church. During the Thatcher era, the Church of England spoke up against Mrs Thatcher and her policies. The Bishop of Durham was quite controversial at the time. I was quite impressed with him. There was another bishop, I think he was the Bishop of Liverpool, who was very critical of the government as indeed the Archbishop of Canterbury was. I thought that was very telling, about how unjust Mrs Thatcher was and how she divided this country, that the Church, a fairly conservative institution itself, felt the need to actually

say that a lot of her policies were fundamentally un-Christian and that she was causing social and economic problems. I think that really impressed me about the Church at that time. I think that it still has such a role today.   *(Ian, Couple 5)*

For some, the Church as an institution was a vehicle that was not really helpful in their search for pastoral care and acceptance of who they were and what they wanted to be for each other. The institutional model of the Church had a tendency to seem remote and rather out of touch. In pastoral need what they sought was not a teaching document nor a pronouncement from above, but an empathic encounter. For them, the Church that was unable to wear a human face was a Church not worthy of the name at all. To that extent some gave a view that might describe the Church as 'its own worst enemy'. On the one hand most had experiences at a personal level that they felt to be affirming and, as we shall see later, empowering. At its most personable, the Church was a gift in their lives that had allowed them to feel less afraid about who they were and what they wanted in seeking a blessing for a faithful partnership. At its worst the Church seemed rather bombastic and judgemental, making remote pronouncements without offering any sort of human engagement. This was the irony of the Church as Steve saw it.

I think I had lost contact with the Church by my teenage years and I regarded it as a rather outmoded, crumbling institution. But I always had this feeling at the back of my mind that God did exist and I found that in moments of crisis I did pray. When I started counselling a few years ago I became aware of a distinction between the 'spiritual' and 'religion' where you must do this and must do that. I saw the Church as rather authoritarian. Now my view has changed somewhat. I have now met people who are interested in human beings as people and can accept them for what they are rather than forcing 'religion' upon them, telling them that they are going to hell because they are gay. I think that by getting involved in St Luke's I have realised that there

> are some real people out there that care for other real
> people. It is just the sort of humanity that is really touching.
> *(Steve, Couple 5)*

Most couples seemed aware of 'two Churches' like this: the one apparently high-handed and remote, the other sometimes appearing as human and compassionate. For the couples interviewed the personal encounter always redeemed the media-presented stereotype of self-styled authoritarianism. Their sense of safety was always secured in the welcome of the local church rather than in the perceived position of the hierarchical Church, a position that seemed to them to do little more than encourage fear and suspicion. The place of the local church in the pastoral encounter was cemented by their testimonies to the warm hospitality they received in what they recognised as quite a cool, if not frosty, general climate.

> I don't think that I have experienced any negative response
> from the local church. All of you at St Luke's have affirmed
> us either through the original blessing or with the subsequent
> renewal services. So my view of St Luke's has never
> changed. I have always loved it and I have got a lot of time
> for it.   *(Douglas, Couple 6)*

Pastoral liturgy and pastoral care. Preparation and good practice

All pastoral liturgy that reflects a rite of passage, whether services of naming for children, or baptism and confirmation, marriage or funerals, demand high levels of integrity from those who conduct them and responsibility from those who prepare for and take part in them. Because the whole area of supporting same-gender couples through services of blessing and covenanted union is still quite a contentious one in certain parts of the wider Church, there is a strong need to be *seen* to be acting with that same sense of integrity and responsibility. The claims of critics that same-gender relationships are fleeting and often promiscuous will only be countered if proper support structures are in place for those that wish to avail themselves of a Christian model that encourages those relationships to be faithful and lasting. In her book on the processes of separation Diane Vaughan shares with the reader the views of same-gender and opposite-gender couples whose partnerships/marriages break down. She notes that gay and lesbian partnerships are often lived out in relative isolation. While break-up and separation is never easy she contends that it is precisely the public nature of commitment that allows the couple to be sustained while together. In the unhappy event of separation or divorce, there is less opportunity to discover support unless that same public witnessing has been put in place at the time of 'coupling'.

> While having a smaller public may reduce the disruption of separation, the benefits should not be considered without weighing possible costs. The fact that others know and acknowledge the relationship creates pressure to try to work things out when people become unhappy. Without public confirmation, a relationship is less stable, more precarious. Should the couple separate, each person will have less support. Who can partners turn to, for example, when their homosexual or married lovers leave them, if no one knows that the relationship exists?[9]

While my principal interest in this book does not lie in the dynamics of marriage and partnership breakdown, those of us engaged in the responsibility of helping people 'couple' (principally through the marriage rite) should be aware of these insights. Marriages do not take place in secret. They are conducted in the hours of daylight with the church doors open, the banns called and the proposed marriage published on the church notice boards. We expect friends and supporters to be invited. In ceremonies of blessing following civil marriage the congregation are invited to give vocal assent to the marriage by doing their best to support the couple in that marriage. Thus support at every level is an important ingredient in the process.

Same-gender couples who make their way to St Luke's for a service of covenanted union and blessing are asked to begin constructing that support by thinking about what they want from life together and reflecting those things in a pastoral liturgy of blessing. This they design with the assistance of the clergy and lay people who have agreed to assist (with the support of the PCC) in a short period of preparation. It is hoped that the couple will have known each other for some time (usually a minimum of one year).

The preparation periods cover four one-hour sessions. The first of these is an open agenda session, the aim of which is to ascertain whether the couple's needs can be met by the kind of ministry and liturgy the church is able to offer. The couples are always asked to go away and think about whether they want to continue with the preparation. In the last five years only two couples have declined. Second, there is consideration about the strengths and weaknesses of each partner and how that can be reflected in the act of blessing. Third, a date is agreed, and a 'gay friendly' printer recommended who will provide service booklets according to the agreed design, as well as a sympathetic solicitor who will help them draft their last will and testament. Fourth, there is a rehearsal for the ceremony. The ceremony is conducted by one of the parish clergy and members of St Luke's congregation staff the service. Fees are charged at the rate recommended by the Church commissioners for a wedding, with the exception of a licence fee. All of this is done to ensure that the event is seen to be taken seriously.

The couples were asked to reflect on what they felt about this process and what it meant to them to take such a level of responsibility for the planning of their service of blessing.

All of them described a feeling of nervousness as they attended their first preparation session and a sense of relief that they could now go beyond a telephone call to a face-to-face meeting. All once more reiterated their delight at being taken seriously as people in relationship with the significance of what was about to be embarked upon recognised.

Oh, I thought it was a very serious thing. This was a very

serious part, which I liked very much. There was nothing superficial and you made us think seriously about what we wanted. I like it very much the way you did it. *(Daniela, Couple 1)*

The first time was a bit nerve-wracking because we didn't know what to expect or what would be expected of us . . . at the end of it all we felt a bit knackered but basically we knew that the outcome would be something that we really wanted. *(Anna, Couple 3)*

I think that we were both nervous at our first meeting but we were soon put at our ease. We found that we were just treated as if we were ordinary regular people. *(Douglas, Couple 6)*

Part of the struggle in preparing for a service of covenanted union and blessing is how to resource the couple. There are liturgies available and a wealth of material that might be borrowed from the United States of America, where the most recent census reports reveal 1.6 million households consisting of partners of the same sex.[10] *The Essential Guide to Lesbian and Gay Weddings*[11] is one typical resource. However, it assumes a context that is not yet a part of the culture here in the United Kingdom. What does and does not constitute marriage is still open for discussion and will form part of this reflection in a later chapter. Meanwhile, couples preparing at St Luke's have to work quite hard at describing what they want to say to God, and to each other before God, in their preparation sessions and in the conversations they have together at home. However, with proper enabling, this can be a liberating experience.

In our first session we were put right on the spot. We said that we wanted to do this service and were immediately asked why. It was just the right question to ask us. What was the meaning behind what we were doing? So the preparation was quite directive to begin with and I think that it had to be in order to give it focus. It made us come up with more precise thoughts and reasons for what we were doing and what we actually wanted out of the service. *(Amelia, Couple 2)*

We valued that. It really did affirm and it put us into a position whereby we had to articulate what we wanted and what it meant. That's actually quite hard for a same-sex couple, unlike a man and a woman who are able to approach the Church and there is just this written protocol for what you go through. For same-sex couples there isn't a protocol and you have a blank piece of paper and initially that was quite scary because we didn't know what to do. *(Ruth, Couple 2)*

Ruth and Amelia proved to be a quite self-resourcing couple, though it was later agreed that it might have been helpful for them not to have had to start from scratch in the totally unfamiliar world of preparing liturgy. This was adopted as an insight for future good practice. However, it is ironic that this act of empowering was in the first instance one that was received reluctantly.

Initially I wanted the Church to tell us what it was that we were going to do. We felt at a loss. There was no procedure to follow, just a blank page. We didn't know of anyone who had gone through a service like this before. *(Amelia and Ruth, Couple 2)*

Their expectation of the Church was, in the first instance, one that described it as directive. They wanted to be told what to do. This is often the cry of Christians within the faith community and critics outside it. The Church is unable to speak with a single voice, they say. Some of the most highly intelligent and able people, who hold significant positions in responsible jobs, want to be told what to think and do when they meet for worship. Such a view of Church is an abdication of responsibility and partnership within it. Furthermore it leaves power in the hands of the few that are willing to take responsibility for it. This in turn can only lead to an unhealthy misrepresentation of the mind of the whole Church, leaving some in the role of active parent, making decisions and dictating the terms, and leaving the greater part of the Church in an infantilised state.

In Chapter Three we saw that the power base at St Luke's was perceived as fairly evenly spread. For Nathaniel, who made this observation, it was one of the attractions of joining the church community. There was representation of all groups at all levels and thus he considered it to be a community of empowerment. What happened to Amelia and Ruth was that when the representatives of the faith community turned the responsibility for preparing a liturgy over to them, they were at first paralysed with this gesture, which did not match their previous perception of the Church; a model of Church that told them what to do. They came to realise that this model had changed. Instead it had become a community of empowerment. The Church had given them the gift of responsibility for creating an act of worship. It was a risk for both them and the Church because it is a genuine empowerment. Ruth and Amelia began to grow from infancy to adulthood as they took on an entirely new responsibility.

> While it would have been better to have had a service to work from after our first meeting we went away and got a lot of literature and there was one particular key text that we used a lot.   *(Amelia, Couple 2)*

Thus empowered, they went about the task of collecting material and developing a theme that would reflect their love of God through each other.

Others spoke well of the time spent in preparation. Time spent in such a way underscored how important this event was not only for them, but also for the Church. The personal contact, the personal attention, attention to detail and a genuine desire to create a welcoming safe and holy space were all reflected in their comments.

> The fact that we were treated like any other couple made

it feel like it was right. Had we been treated differently and we didn't have to attend as many preparation sessions as other couples then it wouldn't have felt like an endorsement of what we were doing.   *(Chris, Couple 4)*

I valued that when there was any emotional disturbance we were having, you sat us down and talked us through. This way you have taken time to get to know what we are like as people, what we like about each other, what annoys us about each other. You have got some form of insight into the way we live. We know that you wouldn't have done this if you had not thought we were strong enough to go through with it. It felt like a thorough preparation. We felt special. *(Anna, Couple 3)*

I found the preparation meetings extremely helpful . . . we didn't feel pressurised to do the homework and because of that we were able to get things done at our own speed. *(Steve, Couple 5)*

We were both struck by how professional the whole thing was. Really quite impressed with that. It was also a social thing. The way you represented and brought in the local community really came across.   *(Ian, Couple 5)*

The period of time spent in preparation was seen by nearly all the couples as a freeing experience rather than as an obstacle course to be negotiated before being allowed to claim the prize of a service in church. The effect of this experience has also enabled the church community to benefit, as it has become a practice that informs the way we care for and prepare those opposite-sex couples who present themselves for marriage in the parish church.

From preparation to public commitment

The importance of the public nature of this commitment cannot be overstated. The couples all stressed the value in seeing their relationship brought into the open for their family and friends. We live in an age where the financial cost of marriage has reached vulgar proportions and couples preparing for marriage are so pressured to present a good show on the day that their preoccupations are too often centred solely on dress and choreography. It is refreshing to meet couples who, though not recognised in law as married, perhaps have something to offer to all partnerships in their approach to vow-making and covenant. On only one occasion have a couple requested a service of blessing in church and not been able to move beyond a discussion about whether one could wear a designer dress and the other a morning suit. They felt, in that instance, that they were unable to proceed at St Luke's and instead explored other avenues.

At this point in the discussion, the couples were asked to reflect on what they remembered of their service of blessing. They were invited to share what had prompted the formation of the service and the effect of the occasion at the time and subsequently. For some it was a mark of authentic expression for the relationship they had come to find themselves in. Christina and Daniela took their vows of commitment in both Italian and English. This enabled them to express in their first language the sentiments that they wanted to convey to each other before translating them for their numerous English-speaking supporters (including members of the PCC, to whom they issued an open invitation). Christina, who has been widowed for many years, was reminded of her wedding day and the strong feelings of unease the day evoked.

> I was telling Dani the other day that when I got married in the Catholic church there was nothing impressed me that day. I had the feeling I was doing something wrong. Maybe I was not in love with my husband. I don't know what it was but I have not good memories. Last year when I was here with Dani in this church was good for me, and she came into my heart all this time that she would be like that.
> (Christina, Couple 1)

Christina finds that the service of commitment has sealed her feelings. After a lifetime in an unhappy and unfulfilled marriage she now feels a certain 'rightness' in the new and quite different style of relationship that she is embarking upon.

For Ruth and Amelia their service of covenanted union seems to have fulfilled needs in them and enabled them to express things that they wanted to clarify with parents, family and close friends. They remember the service as one that offered clarity to the congregation. There was a moment of welcome when the congregation was advised about the contents of the service and reminded of its purpose. The congregation was encouraged to be a participating group, acting as witnesses to the vows and covenant that were being made before them. Thus they remembered it as an act of witness that was inclusive and engaging. Those in attendance could not then later declare themselves as merely interested observers or ignorant that the two had declared their faithful intent to each other and their desire to be recognised as a covenanting couple. The whole congregation declared their support both by their presence and their active participation. Amelia and Ruth described the purpose and design of the liturgy. For them it was a description of what they felt for each other and how they hoped that those who witnessed the ceremony and their life together would continue to perceive them.

> Helping write the service gave us structure, but aside from the service it gave meaning to our feelings for one another. It really helped us articulate how we feel about each other. *(Amelia, Couple 2)*

> Also how we expect our nearest and dearest to respect that and accept that just because we are two women it should have no lesser effect on them than if their daughter or cousin were marrying a man. I think that the words we used reflected that. *(Ruth, Couple 2)*

> I remember it as being a very serious thing. It was taken very seriously. *(Amelia, Couple 2)*

Anna and Karen found that taking responsibility for the service revealed their ability to bond well over a very important matter.

> We felt like it catered for us. We had a big part to play in it instead of simply slotting into some kind of pre-packaged thing. *(Anna, Couple 3)*

> It was personal but we had to take some sort of responsibility for the fact that it happened. We had to sort out practical details and it all helped because we were so nervous. It meant that we had to pull together and work together not only for the service but in life too. *(Karen, Couple 3)*

Paul and Chris had been keen to blend a service that had some personal touches but maintained a strong 'traditional' element to it. So, although the form of service they created was neither a duplicate of the marriage service nor one that borrowed heavily from it, there was still a framework that their congregation would recognise. Because they were able to do this, it meant that they could design both something that they would find meaningful and descriptive of their relationship before God, and also something they could actually live up to.

> The personal side of us actually preparing it was very mean-ingful for us and for everybody else. A lot of people said it was the best one they had ever been to because they knew how much work we had put in to it. We could not have wished for it to have been any better than it was. *(Paul, Couple 4)*

> Also because we kept some tradition, but brought in the vows. We worked hard on getting the vows right – probably more on that than anything else, but that is something that other couples very often don't get the opportunity to do. So we wrote those vows knowing that we were going to stick by those vows. Because we wrote them I think that it helped us more to mean what we were saying. *(Chris, Couple 4)*

Most couples found the opportunity to be creative in their service of worship a liberating experience. Whereas it might be assumed that the opportunity to write personal vows and declarations of intent was little more than a licence to dilute lifelong faithfulness, nothing could be further from the truth. In the already quoted *Marriage after Modernity*, Adrian Thatcher cites Malcolm Johnson, an Anglican priest, who for many years supported same-gender couples by offering services of covenant and blessing. Johnson declares that when couples first came to meet him he would offer them the opportunity to make temporary vows to each other rather as those entering religious orders and communities might make temporary vows before lifelong vows. None of those he suggested this idea to were interested in anything other than a lifelong commitment.[12] I have to say that this has been my own experience, so much so that I have long since given up making the offer. Steve and Ian chose to reflect their faithfulness in this covenant service by dispensing with an exchange of rings and instead presenting each other with copies of the Bible – a mark of God's covenant. For them it was important to be free of what they saw as materialistic distractions in order to focus on what they had to say before God.

> We watched this marriage programme on Channel 5 and there was a lot of money being thrown at conventions, hiring halls and cars and the such like. We were able to dispense with a lot of that. *(Ian, Couple 5)*

> Yes, it was personal to us but there were guidelines, but because we were able to have our say it was very helpful. Instead of paying lip service to something which could have happened in a conventional wedding, we designed something of which we felt a part. *(Steve, Couple 5)*

> I think that at the end of the day the actual church service is the most important bit. The other stuff can submerge that in a conventional wedding. What does it matter if you go to

church on a bicycle? The actual important thing is the vows. *(Ian, Couple 5)*

The couples reveal that the reason they approach the Church for blessing and affirmation is because in this creative liturgical service they seek an opportunity to clarify publicly the integrity of their sexual identity and their sense of faithfulness in a societal climate of uncertainty and some hostility. They seek an opportunity to express their purpose in wanting to share their life together and their intention to do this openly and within an environment of stability and trust. They further wish to be seen as responsible citizens, taking the steps of offering vows to each other before God and declaring a lasting intention for their union together in the absence of a legal framework to support and protect them. They ask their family, their friends and the Christian faith community to take them seriously and they ask that all this be done within a sanctified environment.

> It was so important for us to describe the love we had for each other, the love we had for our friends and our love for God and thanks too for God letting us be together. *(Stephen, Couple 6)*

> Yes, it was so nice to have the free will to be ourselves and not have to pretend. *(Doug, Couple 6)*

The church community of Chapter Two reflected upon itself and perceived the models of hospitality, sanctuary and empowerment, and these models seem to be reflected in its ministry as revealed in these testimonies. In the next chapter we will see how these offers of welcome, safety and freedom allow both couples and congregation to find common ground in their understanding of what it means to convey and receive 'blessing'.

CHAPTER 5

Voices in Harmony

practice and partnership
what does it mean to be 'blessed'?

Chapters Three and Four have introduced us to the principal voices in this narrative. The church community has begun to reflect upon an experience that some recall and others have had passed down to them. Using many voices it has been an important activity to recover the original story of Rodney and Saxon. This has been the key story that has informed the developing attitude of a church membership looking to reflect responsibly upon a ministry to same-gender couples. It is particularly informative to their understanding of what it means to support this ministry with a service of blessing and covenant. The voices of the couples have entered the narrative in a different way. They are the recipients of the church's ministry. It is they who come looking to be served and affirmed and it is from this perspective that they speak. Theirs is an experience that is not a direct connection to the story of Rodney Madden and Saxon Lucas. Except for one couple, none claim knowledge of the events that surrounded the 'controversial' services in 1979 and in 1985. They speak instead of an experience that is born of the effects of those events shaped over a 20-year period. Those voices confirm the finding of a church that welcomed them, made them feel safe and empowered them to express their desire to be in faithful partnership before God and the Church.

In this chapter the two sets of voices interact in the narrative. Whilst not quite a dialogue, they face and explore similar questions, providing each other with insights from their different perspectives. Members of the congregation begin to address the level of their involvement in issues of same-sex blessings. This begins with a review of how conscious they are that the support for same-gender couples still continues and looks generally at what they think of such couples forming partnerships. The voices of the couples also speak, naming their own consciousness of the ministry at St Luke's and what difference it has made to them. Finally all voices share their thoughts on what it means to be blessed.

There is little doubt that in 1979 the entire congregation at St Luke's knew what was happening to them; press coverage and some local interest made that so. However, 20 years have elapsed and much of the localised sensationalism has died away. Instead there remains a story of legend-like character and a slow drift of couples who come from nearby to pledge themselves in lifelong unions.

The couples are in no doubt that the Church is a complex institution and this does not make it easy to approach. Most of them talked about being nervous. Two couples described a past experience of the Church as 'frightening'. All of them were aware that the Church of England has multifarious views on gay and lesbian relations and so all took great care in making their approach. The ministry at St Luke's became part of their consciousness either because they had attended a service of blessing on a previous occasion, or the information was passed to them by word of mouth, or they contacted an agency like the Lesbian and Gay Christian Movement or Gay Switchboard. Amelia and Ruth read about it in a magazine.

> We did a lot of research in terms of looking at particular churches, and church organisations as well. When we first thought that we actually wanted to have the ceremony in church of course we had no idea of where to go or what to do. We went to lots of different places and then we read an article on St Luke's in one of the newspaper weekend magazines. It spoke of the previous vicar and how he had been kicked out for doing gay marriages. Then it dawned

> on us that we knew the place. So we decided to make contact. *(Ruth, Couple 2)*

So, for the couples, the awareness of the St Luke's story is vague, but it is brought to their consciousness by knowing where to go to find out. What this tells us is that even if the particular church story of Rodney and Saxon does not live as a wider community story, the consequences of that story and its effect on the lives of those who minister at St Luke's is held in a discreet oral tradition. It is also marked on the records of 'safe' agencies seeking to serve same-gender couples. In other words, people in the wider community who need to know or want to find out can access the information. It is a quietly held community story.

For the senior members of the church community (C1), the personal experience with Rodney and Saxon remained their reference point when thinking about whether the blessing of such unions continues. It is still a way of identifying the church story with what they feel the Christian message is and how that is demonstrated in pastoral action. A service of blessing for Rodney and Saxon was a point of entry into the community for that couple and a way of offering affirmation and acceptance. Most in this category referred to knowing Rodney and Saxon as their principal, if not sole, experience of a relationship with a gay couple. With 20 years between the event of their union and this period of reflection it was clear that the memory of this event had been a powerful binding factor for them. Some declared that they were not happy at the time, but had come to recognise a wider societal change that had vindicated not only the initiative of the priest at the time but also their decision to support it. Though none spoke of their involvement in the preparations for the service of blessing there was a sense now in which they shared in some ownership of the legend as they relayed it. When in 1985 Saxon and Rodney had a second service to celebrate their twenty-fifth anniversary, there was clearly more obvious and widespread involvement. Lavinia was a churchwarden at the time. She was kept informed of the original events and of any subsequent blessings that took place. She knew what the practice of St Luke's was in those days, but is uncertain as to what it is now.

> Then I guess the rector wound his neck out and did it if he believed that couples were genuine and reported it to the PCC more subsequently than before the event. But at the time I was Churchwarden he always did take us into his confidence about it. I think that he was victimised in lots of ways and attacked because of it. He did believe that he was doing the right thing and I certainly did. I had no qualms about supporting him. What happens now, I am a bit unsure. *(Lavinia, C1)*

There is likely to be a problem if levels of discretion reach the point of making the thing a secret. This is a good argument for extending the involvement of the laity in the pastoral practice of preparing same-gender couples for services of blessing and covenanted union. Rodney and Saxon emerged from a recognised church community as known faces, to make vows of commitment to each other. Not only did their ceremony take place before their priest and family and friends, it was a part of the life of the local church community. The community of faith ministered with its priest to the couple. This is a much more powerful statement of ministry than the one which grants permission for the priest to discern and decide alone. What makes the first model powerful is that it is a statement of solidarity in ministry. The second is a statement of support: 'You do it and we will back you up.' Rather than being backed in a ministerial initiative that the priest otherwise does alone, if *the priesthood of the baptised community* was released by owning the action of the pastoral practice then the responsibility for it would be more equally shared. Furthermore, it would be difficult to dismiss it and demonise a single individual, as was amply illustrated in the weekend newspaper magazine article read by Amelia and Ruth. Church members here seem to be suggesting that for the sake of openness this might be a direction toward which St Luke's needs to move. Currently few are sure as to what happens, when and how often.

I am sure it *used* to go on but people were very discreet about things.   *(James, C1)*

Oh I *think* it is a continuing thing. I think that is how it will be.   *(Jennifer, C1)*

I would say that it is a part of the present — *hopefully.* *(Doreen, C1)*

Only Millie (C1), who didn't know Saxon and Rodney, was able to confirm that the current church practice maintains a continuity of ethos with the practice described in the original story. She declared that there needed to be understanding on the part of the church community, and the commitment and desire to make a lasting relationship on the part of those couples seeking the Church's ministry and God's blessing.

I have only attended one blessing as a sidesperson. I understand that it is to make vows of commitment, love and
understanding to each other, rather like a heterosexual
wedding with family and friends witnessing their promises
to each other and the priest giving the blessing.   *(Millie,
C1)*

A similar degree of uncertainty prevailed amongst the inter-mediates. None of them were entirely sure as to what the current practice is though all speculated that there was a continuing practice. This is further reason now to explore ways of encouraging greater transparency for this ministry to same-sex couples. Who was responsible for facilitating this ministry? There was further uncertainty: Moira thought it was the clergy. June and Arthur named it as an unidentified 'they' who do it; Mary and Sally named 'St Luke's' as the source of encouragement of commitment. Nobody was able to be precise or to utilise personal language.

When the newest members of the congregation were asked what they knew about the support of same-gender couples there was almost universal agnosticism about current practice. Either because they had not had sufficient time to catch the story, or because it was unimportant to them or, most likely, because it is not a high-profile ministry within the church and so it was not something that they were distinctly aware of. Only Nathaniel seemed to know about it because he was on the PCC and went out of his way to find out. Those representing ethnic minorities displayed a similar level of knowledge. This was markedly in contrast with the young people of St Luke's. They were not only confident in knowing that the practice of support for same-gender couples was current in the ministerial life of the church, they addressed their comments in a way quite different from any other section of the church community. As members of the congregation it was something that they saw themselves as a part of. It was not something that St Luke's did, or the clergy did. It was not a pet ministry or specialist interest of one or two individuals in the church. It was something that they knew about and owned up to being linked with and acknowledged ownership of.

> It is something that we do.   (*Emily, C5*)

> It is a good thing to do, but not many churches do it.
> (*Alex, C5*)

> I have heard that *we* do them, because my mum went to one.   (*Nicola, C5*)

These are the inheritors of the Rodney and Saxon legend. They have caught the spirit of the story in a way that perhaps their more seasoned Christian elders have been slower to discover for themselves and express to others. The story is not simply a thing of the past that has no association with the present. The recovery or remembering of such a story always has consequences for the present and usually, if we are honest, has an effect upon our lives. Whatever else it does, it ensures that nothing is ever quite the same again.

With this in mind, members of the congregation began to move away from the specific story that they had been able to retrieve and how conscious they were of the pastoral ministry for same-gender couples in the church. Reflecting instead on what they thought about gay and lesbian relationships in general and whether such relationships were best modelled in stable partnerships, they began to identify and think about some core issues. Central themes such as stability and faithfulness emerge. These are themes that are echoed by the voices of the couples, who similarly seek security and wholeness. Many of them testified to what a difference the encounter with the local church and a service of blessing made to their lives. Perhaps the most striking feature of the congregational responses lay in *how* they chose to express their thinking. Some answered in abstract terms, others recalled personal experiences and were able to speak of friendships they had with gay men and lesbian women, and some had formed friendships with couples. The tone of all answers was mainly warm and accepting, but in the case of those who declared themselves to have gay and lesbian friends this was particularly so.

Senior church members described a general scene of what life had been like for their generation on this issue. Same-gender couples openly living together, let alone having their relationships blessed in church, were situations that were considered shocking to the culture and context of the day.

> Well, being that much older than many of the people concerned it was rather a shock to see this *(presumably the open service of blessing)* happening. Before it had always been very much a cloak and dagger affair . . . but I certainly feel that if two people are sufficiently attracted to make a stable relationship then it is important. *(James, C1)*

The openness at the time of the first service of blessing had brought with it a degree of pain for some members of St Luke's though they identify this principally with the adverse publicity from press coverage. Coping with what was then a radical model of ministry had been somewhat stressful. Others pointed out that the increased degree of openness amongst gay and lesbian couples led to an alteration of the climate at that time. All agreed that to be a good thing. What seems to have been true in 1979 was that Saxon and Rodney arriving at St Luke's confronted many with their own prejudices and enabled a process of thinking to start. For many of those who could remember them personally this was clearly a major watershed.

Faithful and stable
Lavinia recalled marvelling at Rodney and Saxon being together for 25 years.

> At the time that Saxon and Rod had their twenty-fifth anniversary I remember saying that it was remarkable. I could not stay married for twenty-five years and so I celebrated that two people were so committed to stay together for that length of time. It is still my view that if they are gay or lesbian or same-sex and they are committed to each other, then I believe that is something to celebrate not condemn.
> (Lavinia, C1)

That faithfulness over such a long period is something to be celebrated not condemned, is echoed by other voices and for Millie it began a positive change of heart on the matter.

> I grew up in a time when homosexuality was frowned upon, but I had broad-minded parents who accepted people for what they were and I give thanks for them teaching me this. As far as same-sex blessings, I must admit it took me time to accept this . . . but it has helped me to realise that homosexual partnerships can be lasting as can any relationship and not casual affairs as in my ignorance I had felt previously. (Millie, C1)

This raises an important issue for all church members reflecting on this topic. Stability in relationships was seen as key and deserving of support. The openness with which the ministry began in 1979 might now be seen to have reaped a reward some 20 years later. More gay people are prepared to be open about their lifestyles. Consequently, more heterosexual men and women are now more likely to consciously have gay and lesbian friends, and quite possibly some that are in steady partnerships. Other members of the church community were able to draw on examples of couples and individuals they had come to know since Rodney and Saxon. June and Moira (C2) had views tempered by personal and more recent experiences. Moira has a friend whose son was gay and who recently died. She had listened to her friend describe her uncertain feelings for the partnership, but in her grief she had become quite close to her deceased son's partner. June has two sets of friends who are in gay partnerships, both long-standing. Knowing someone personally who was either openly gay or lesbian and single or in a same-gender partnership seemed to alter the tone with which the church members spoke on the matter.

In a small book on Christian same-sex partnerships Jeffrey John looks at the issue of promiscuity and fidelity. A number of his conclusions are borne out by the observations of those interviewed at St Luke's.

> It is a testimony to the reality and strength of the mono-gamous instinct in all human beings that gay relationships succeed despite the lack of any legal framework or social support . . . [1]

Members of the church community in each of the group listings but in particular C1, C2 and C3 lent support for this view, some having a degree of experience of such relationships. Jeffrey John continues:

> . . . there are at least two special factors which make homo-sexual men statistically more promiscuous than heterosexuals. The first is in the absence of opportunities in ordinary life for meeting other gay people, and without accepted social structures within which 'courting' can take place. [2]

The couples corroborate his view. Each was asked whether a service in church had made a difference to their relationship. Every couple said that it had. Many spoke of their sense of insecurity in gay relationships prior to meeting their partner. Often this had been debilitating and flew in the face of the stability they had been looking for. Chris and Paul offer a good example.

> I am not sure that having a blessing has changed our relationship apart from actually making us feel more secure.   *(Paul, Couple 4)*

> I think it fair to say that Paul was quite lacking in security in the early stages of our relationship and that tended to be more to do with bad relationships in the past. So, yes, it helped to endorse the commitment we were making to each other.   *(Chris, Couple 4)*

> Plus we were not sort of jumping at it. I didn't keep on at Chris to say that this was what I wanted. I wanted him to do it because he wanted to. Then I would know that we would be together in it.   *(Paul, Couple 4)*

Church members across the spectrum also identified a need to encourage faithfulness in relationships because it was seen as a healthy and stabilising social factor, while instability was seen as a feature of casual relating, the 'one night stand'. To some extent, the development of a service of covenanted union and blessing for same-gender couples might go some way towards addressing that. Eric Marcus, in a research survey of over 50 same-gender couples, explores the theme of faithfulness and stability in a chapter called 'Commitment'. He recalls the commitment ceremony he and his partner undertook and notes for whom it is of particular importance.

> When my partner and I had a commitment ceremony, two years after we first met, our ceremony made a difference in two ways: first, we both felt more profoundly committed and secure after we had exchanged vows in front of our families and friends. Second, the ceremony changed how supported

we felt in our relationship by our friends and family who treated us differently after we'd made a public commitment.[3]

While it is impossible to argue that the activity of a same-gender blessing ceremonial of itself makes a couple more faithful and stable, the voices of the couples attending St Luke's were unanimous that it *had* made a difference to them. Paul and Chris identified how it met their fear of insecurity and acted as a kind of catalyst to build their confidence with each other. For Ruth and Amelia, it met a similar fear, but gave some structure to their life together by formalising it.

> I'm quite an insecure person so it has made me feel more secure in our relationship. It's not that I think that Amelia is going to run away. However I need some form of stability that I can grab hold of and I know for a fact that if I was heterosexual I would be married to somebody I would be sharing the *whole* of my life with. I would never have chosen just to have lived together because it was a cool and trendy thing to do. I need some formalisation of things. It was very important for both of us and it made me realise that this is it. This is for me. This is for Amelia. This is it until the curtain comes down. *(Ruth, Couple 2)*

For Daniela it heightens her sense of responsibility and commitment.

> I think it has made some kind of difference. I didn't think that it could change anything, but I think I feel more responsible now, so it must have changed me somehow. Feeling more attached in a way, in some ways. More responsible, more committed. *(Daniela, Couple 1)*

For Steve, his appreciation of his partner has been raised. He knew that he always valued him before but since the service of covenanted union and blessing it seems even more significant.

> I think that it has made us more aware of us being a couple. The preparation helped with that. We knew that it was

> something that we wanted to do together as a couple. It has made me more aware of the dynamics in our relationship as well. Ever since the blessing I feel that I have come even closer to Ian. *(Steve, Couple 5)*

For his partner it has been a time of real strengthening. Not only did the preparation and the ceremony sow seeds of faith in Ian in which he felt affirmed and accepted, the act of commitment in front of friends (some of whom were gay and surprised at his decision to come to church), was sustaining.

> I think that it has made us stronger. Since the summer we had encountered a fair number of problems really. There was trouble for me at work, which became very depressing, and there has been stuff for Steve which has been very demanding and taken up a lot of time. I feel that we have been strengthened because of this and despite those problems, but I think that is what taking the vows is all about. It is sticking with each other through thick and thin. The problems and the joys, that is what life is all about. *(Ian, Couple 5)*

The couples thus testify that in each case a service of blessing made a notable difference to some aspect of their life together. Members of St Luke's congregation encountered in Rodney and Saxon the experience of a couple who had been together for 19 years *before* their service of blessing. While the members were unable to verify that Saxon and Rodney felt different during or after a service of blessing, they were able to declare that the service of blessing in 1979 and their service of thanksgiving in 1985 did effect some change in them as a congregation. It might be argued that the value of such ceremonies lies as much in the congregation making a statement of intention as in the couple declaring their love and commitment. Those who witness are asked to declare their support for the couple. What they witness is a change in status for the couple albeit one that goes unrecognised in law. A number of church members identified this as a need for a sense of loving support to undergird the stability of such relationships.

The discussion amongst the congregation prompted personal disclosure from some that was particularly significant. They had already declared themselves to have good friendships with gay and lesbian people, some of whom were in faithful partnerships. This moment in the reflection process revealed that two more had close experiences with same-sex couples and gave examples of not just friends but of *members of their own family* in faithful same-sex partnerships. Sara (C3) spoke of an uncle in a relationship of 12 years standing. She had known since she was a child of ten and had therefore grown up with this degree of openness. Such is her confidence that she is similarly open about him with her own children. They often go to stay with John and Jim and although George, her young son, doesn't fully understand what it means for the two men to live in partnership, he knows that they are a bit different. The discovery of gay and lesbian people in our own families will have a profound effect on our commitment to loving support and on how we find a language with which to talk to the children of our families and communities about same-sex affection and stable relationships. For some of the couples this was a critical insight. Being in a same-gender relationship did not absolve them from their desire to be in a loving wider family and to share responsibility within it. For many, being open with parents or with children is a difficult encounter. For others it is a path they have already begun to walk, sometimes with pleasing results.

> Our families are very much involved and they saw our cere-
> mony as a marriage. So it's all about the people who are
> nearest and dearest to us. They all saw it as a marriage.
> Both our parents would introduce the other person as 'my
> daughter in law'. Always.   *(Ruth, Couple 2)*

Amongst the members of the congregation it was an important admission by Mary that 20 years before, she and her husband had supported Saxon and Rodney in person but made child-minding arrangements for their very young children on the day. Perhaps a more open climate even 20 years ago might have seen her bring them to the service as indeed others did. Sara tells of Jim and John having a good model of faithful relationship. She has other gay and lesbian friends in long-term partnerships.

> I know some people in long-standing partnerships. Some of them are the most responsible adults I know. If my children grew up to be as good and responsible as they are, then I would be happy.   *(Sara, C3)*

> My sister is a lesbian and she has been living with this partner for years and they bought a house and so on and it is much like any other marriage really.   *(Daisy, C3)*

Stability affects us at every level of society and Daisy, in a throw-away remark, identifies this. Her view is that gay and lesbian partners should be afforded the same opportunities as others for stability in their partnerships. It is a wholesome feature of life for them *but it also does something for her too*. When her friends and relations have stability in *their* lives this has a percolating effect for her and possibly the whole family. This suggestion is powerful in indicating that how we live and conduct our private lives, whilst remaining an individual liberty, does have some effect on those around us at different societal levels. It may be argued on the strength of this alone that each responsible society should try to create an infrastructure that allows all individuals a degree of security and stability precisely because its whole structure will benefit from it, and this clearly applies to gay and lesbian couples. Furthermore, if a Church institution or any local church is to take an active and responsible role in shaping that kind of stable societal structure it will have to look at positive ways of engaging with gay and lesbian couples in its ministry of welcome and affirmation. Exactly what form that should take remains part of the open discussion in the congregation and there were some who were uncertain as to what it might be.

This language of love took a different turn amongst some of those who were most undecided in their views on gay and lesbian partnerships. Two in particular declared a need to be open and non-judgemental. Roger (and his wife Susannah, a non-interviewee) had been victims of church judgement in a previous parish. When it was discovered that they were living together prior to marriage, they felt judged and distanced. This experience clearly wounded him quite deeply and it becomes one that guides his comments. Discernment, he declared, was not the same as judgement and he felt that the Church was not best served in its pastoral ministry when it adopted the model of Judge.

> There are lots of things that the Church appears to jump to conclusions and to judge people. I personally think that the role of judging people is best done elsewhere.   *(Roger, C3)*

If the principal work of the Church is seen to be to render judgement then the image of Church as Judge will be the prevailing image. There will be undoubted consequences for its pastoral ministry should the Church cultivate such a singular image. Distancing was the wounding that Roger and Susannah experienced in a church community that passed judgement on their pre-marital cohabitation. This sense of 'not fitting in' is a common experience for gay and lesbian couples too.

> The local church round the corner from where I live basically shuns me, whereas we can come to St Luke's and be welcomed as a couple. Being seen as a couple at St Luke's is not a problem.   *(Chris, Couple 4)*

The cultivating of any stability in relationships for same-gender couples needs to take note of the disadvantage such couples already experience. The youth (C5) noted that the social climate discriminated against gay and lesbian couples because it was one that adopted a predominantly heterosexual perspective. Some of them had experience of the disabling nature of discrimination in areas of sex and ethnicity, either for themselves or amongst their friends. It was a very formative experience for these young teenagers and powerfully attested to.

> I am black and female and while I have not experienced prejudice directly, I know of others who have. It happens particularly in the work place. You see it in the media too. So I can see that gay people are a kind of minority and I would say that now is the time to be understanding it.
> *(Nicola, C5)*

What seems conclusively true is that if the heterosexual perspective becomes the only perspective then society never has to answer questions about same-gender attraction and partnerships: it has effectively hidden them. The young people saw this in what they described as an issue of 'difference'. Tom (C5) noted that there was significant difference in the way men and women related to each other from the way men and men and women and women did. What the heterosexual social perspective has done is to set opposite-sex relations as the benchmark for all relations. This I find convincing, particularly in dealing with the suggestion that the support of same-gender partnership ceremonies somehow diminishes the institution of marriage. Others in the youth category (C5) thought that gay and lesbian couples had to work harder at 'proving' themselves a *bona fide* couple. This was a view in sympathy with many of the couples themselves.

> For me, our life together is a marriage but we have to work harder at it because our relationship is unusual. Because we don't have a marriage licence we have to make the vows mean more.   *(Stephen, Couple 6)*

To support this the church young people adopted the language of *liberty*. Stable partnerships were a *right* not a *privilege*.

> Any individual has got the right to form a stable partnership, whether they are straight or gay.   *(Daniel, C5)*

The language of liberty is not dissimilar to the language of empowerment used to describe the local church community in Chapter Three and the influence of its ministry as outlined in parts of Chapter Four. It proved to be a consistent image of how members of St Luke's church community saw themselves and their task in pastoral ministry. An ethos of empowerment is most likely to fit with the language of liberty. What remains to be seen is whether such language translates into pastoral action.

Often it is difficult to ascertain how much a personal viewpoint is influenced by a particular situation or by wider national and sometimes global influences. The church community at St Luke's having thought about gay and lesbian couples in general and how they viewed the experience of stable partnerships being endorsed and blessed within the Church, began to think and comment on how much the local church experience had contributed to that change. Perhaps unsurprisingly the senior and intermediate members resourced themselves with the personal recollections of the principal story at their disposal. This was of primary import-ance. They accepted that 20 years earlier there had been a mood of change in society at large, but that it was individual stories like the one they now held for St Luke's that had enabled that change to have its greatest impact upon them. The experience brought about by the service of blessing for Rodney and Saxon and the high level of press coverage it attracted had clearly proved difficult for some of them. However, with hindsight they had seen the value of the experience and it had drawn out what can only be described as a 'generosity of spirit'. One person stated quite poignantly that to have watched Rodney and Saxon take their vows 'from a distance' would have been condescending and done no more than throw up the obvious question, 'Is this right?'

It is a question that the wider Church has continued to argue over for the last 20 years. Bishop Frank Griswold calls this the Gamaliel Principle, outlining it in an article *Naming and Living the Mystery.*[4] He explains this principle with reference to the speech of Gamaliel to the Sanhedrin in the Acts of the Apostles.[5]

> So, in the present case I tell you, keep away from these men and let them alone; because if this plan or this undertaking is of human origin, it will fail; but if it is of God, you will not

be able to overthrow them — in that case you may even be found fighting against God.

Griswold's point is a simple one. There are occasions when it is only possible to advance a debate that has become stuck by enabling the experience to happen and then spending time reflecting upon it to discern the mind of Christ. For a number of senior and intermediate members this had been an important experience and a number of them noted their change of heart as a result of it.

> My views have certainly changed. Being in close proximity with what was happening has made my views change. *(James, C1)*

> Oh yes . . . I have had the chance to see partnerships in practice, been able to talk about it and understand more. I think I am quite broad-minded and open, but I have become more so. *(Millie, C1)*

> My views have changed in so far as the gay/lesbian issue hadn't really come home to me before . . . and of course when I came to St Luke's it was there as an issue and part of life and friends and community. *(Mary, C2)*

Others felt that their views had been changed but as a result of what they considered to be other influences. One felt challenged by her children who had brought home with them new perspectives on life as they were growing up. Another felt that he was in the process of change.

> I think it probably has changed a little but not a lot . . . I am probably slightly more towards the possibility of same-sex blessings, but I am still not fully decided. *(Roger, C3)*

Lavinia (C1) declared her views of 25 years to be confirmed rather than changed. She noted a greater degree of openness, both in the Church and elsewhere. Furthermore, she noted that some of this openness may have influenced legal changes granting greater civil liberty for gay and lesbian people. What she inadvertently raises is a question concerning the dynamics of change. How does law become law and what are the criteria for and moments of reform for law? A number of ethnic minority members were less happy about blessing same-gender couples in church because they perceived that it took them outside what they thought to be the law of the Church. Some declared that if the laws changed then it would be alright, St Luke's could then go ahead with the services of blessing.

However, it would seem that of itself legislation never influences the mood and behavioural changes of society. Instead law has a tendency to *reflect* a societal mood. What is clear here is that this mood has certainly changed since Saxon and Rodney made their vows 20 years ago, but to what extent that change has occurred because of the Saxon and Rodney story (and others like it) remains an open question.

What does a blessing of same-gender partners actually mean?

> There are homosexual couples who grow steadily in fidelity and mutual caring, understanding and support, whose partnerships are a blessing to the world around them . . .[6]

When the bishops of the Church of England published their discussion document *Issues in Human Sexuality* in 1991 this statement was included in the final report. It was one of the most positive statements made about gay and lesbian couples in the document and certainly one that has already been confirmed by the views of those who took part in the preparation of this book. It leads us to a shift of emphasis. This is in order to determine what each 'voice' understands by the term 'blessing'. If couples living faithfully together can be a blessing to those around them, in what way are they seen to be a blessing? Just what does it mean to be 'blessed'? This chapter will go on to explore how this notion of blessing affects each person's thinking either as gay men and lesbian women in partnerships, or as members of a congregation engaged in a ministry of support with gay men and lesbian women.

Questions raised will ask whether a ceremony of blessing compares in any way to the marriage service. Does it need to? Do the couples or church members see any moral or other authority implied in the activity of blessing? The experience of the couples will be drawn on, and they will be asked what, if anything, has changed for them in the experience. Members of the congregation will be invited to reflect on what blessing is, when it is to be conferred and whether they think that it will have any power to change or enhance the relationship that has been blessed.

We begin to enter the realms of definitive religious language. It is a language that most of us living in a Western European or North American culture tend not to use as everyday vocabulary. Thus to engage adequately with the language of 'blessing' was a struggle for most of those who took part. Like a lot of religious language, when deployed in a cultural context that is highly scientific and technological it does not carry a ring of confidence or authenticity. Yet in terms of the ministry of support to gay and lesbian people, it is the area that is most emotive. Many perceive a ceremony of blessing as a means of condoning a way of life and sexual practice that either they are uncertain of or they disapprove of entirely. Thus services of blessing are seen in some parts of the Church as rewards to the undeserving. Often churches offering such a service of blessing stand accused of undermining marriage and family life or making a mockery of them. Couples themselves occasionally see it as some form of touchstone which will strengthen their relationship, or simply as a sign of affirmation in a world in which they feel isolated and invisible. For me it speaks volumes for a Church that is held in scant regard by a wider society much of the time, that it attracts so much attention here and that the ceremony of blessing is so disturbing for some. What is it about blessing (in people's consciousness) that causes this?

Blessing and the language of marriage

There is a plurality of views in the gay and lesbian community about whether their partnerships should ever reflect marriages, or anything that is moulded by a predominantly heterosexual society. Some might declare this to be part of the sexual revolution of counter culture. If heterosexual relationships are the paradigm set within most world cultures, then it is one that is perceived to be in need of resistance. Other lifestyles are to be expressed as representative of a multifarious world culture. Many of the couples arriving at St Luke's found that to be an experience that they were very familiar with. They had friends who were in open disagreement with what they had embarked upon.

> I have had this discussion with loads of people. My two friends Christopher and Darren totally disagree with the idea of same-sex marriage. They don't think it is normal for same-sex couples. *(Karen, Couple 3)*

> Sonia and her friend are lesbians and they are unbelievers and they were surprised that we were actually having a service in church to start with – and Douglas as well, and he even said what a good service it was afterwards. *(Ian, Couple 5)*

However, what is clear is that all couples arriving at St Luke's are from within a perceived minority of the gay and lesbian community. This is firstly because they seek a public ceremony to mark their coupling, secondly because they have come to church for this ceremony, and thirdly because they all speak the language of life-long commitment to their partnership. Thus it is quite difficult *not* to slip into the language of marriage. There is no other common language so readily accessible for people who live on the edge of, or outside church community life.

Amongst the couples, one person was uncomfortable with the term 'marriage' because it had connotations of a male/female partnership. Ian (Couple 5) saw the relationship as a close partnership sealed with vows, but he was at pains to say that he in no way saw it as a second-rate relationship because of this. It was to be something just as valued as a conventional marriage. Ian's partner Steve supported this view, but recognised that even for the guests at the ceremony, the language of marriage was the only language that they could relate to.

> There is a temptation to call it a marriage and several of the guests invited did refer to it as a wedding and meant it as such. I would like to be married and it would be marvellous if everyone would recognise us because I think that gay people are treated differently from straight people. Since the ceremony I certainly feel short-changed by society, but not by the Church. *(Steve, Couple 5)*

Every other couple who took part in the reflection exercise saw their relationship following the service of covenanted union as a marriage or something they could describe in marriage language.

A similar problem occurred for members of the congregation facing the same question. Everyone struggled to find an adequate language with which to discuss services of covenanted union and blessing for those in same-gender partnerships. As with Ian and Steve there was some genuine uneasiness about the use of marital language because it carried with it a status in law that might be misleading to the couples themselves and to the kind of statement the local church was making to the wider Church. For some of the ethnic minority members (C4), there was lack of clarity as to how the local church perceived the status of the ceremonies. Could they be called 'marriage' in any sense of the word? If so, the general unease with the concept was to do with the tradition that had been passed on to them. One member appealed to a scriptural interpretation depicting the creation of God as a design for men and women. However, another defined the services of blessing and covenant as 'a kind of guide', implying that the act of blessing is a means by which God reveals a way in which life might be lived. This was a helpful insight that was later picked up by one couple in particular. There were others who displayed greater comfort using the language of marriage without claiming the status of marriage. Mary makes the distinction between this legal apparatus and what she considers happens before God in the sacrament of marriage.

> I think I can see this as something like a marriage. You are effectively doing the same thing. I suppose the difficulty is if you start to talk about marriage as a civil ceremony that can take place anywhere. I don't think that there the moral question arises, but if you compare it with a church wedding, no matter what the couple themselves may feel towards God, if you have celebrated a marriage in church you are talking about a sacrament. Something has occurred that is irrevocable before God. If the couple happens to be of the same sex and they can't go through the civil pattern, that doesn't make it different. *(Mary, C2)*

Mary, perhaps inadvertently, makes an important theological point here. First she reminds us that a prominent and important feature of Anglican self-understanding has been that it exists as a Church to serve even those who remain outside it. Thus it is possible for a couple seeking heterosexual marriage, one of whom is a self-declared atheist, to marry within the Church of England so long as they fulfil the residency requirements. This makes it all the more ironic that we have such difficulty in supporting, affirming and blessing same-sex couples in church – even when both partners are believers of some description or practising Christians belonging to a faithful church community. Second she has described an understanding of grace that is central to Anglican faith and is supported in the thinking of the Roman Catholic theologian, Karl Rahner. Although Mary describes the dispensing of grace through a sacrament of the Church, Rahner's view of the world is that all is graced and that God's love is shared even outside the vehicle of the Church. Thus, even a non-believer can be a recipient of God's grace. I will return to this in greater detail later.

With members of the church community struggling to find

appropriate religious language it is no surprise that many of the couples had the same difficulty. However, without any obvious access to sacramental or other religious language each couple attempted to describe what made their union like a marriage. Much of that descriptive language utilised terms that one would search for in a serious covenant theology.

> Yes, absolutely. I do see it as a marriage. It is something for life. It is permanent, it's a partnership, it's an agreement, it's two people living together working things out. It's a contract as well. The vows that we took I believe in wholeheartedly . . . they were not taken lightly. The vows were in the truest sense of the word, so yes I do see it as a marriage.   *(Amelia, Couple 2)*

> I feel like we have married two lives and two families.
> *(Ruth, Couple 2)*

The language of the marriage ceremony (the author writes from within the Anglican tradition) defines the importance of marriage (whether one views it as a sacrament or not – and there is some difference of opinion amongst Anglicans), as one that engages the couple at three levels of responsibility. The estate of marriage enables the couple firstly to take their place in the community as a new unit declaring themselves as partners in a new way of life. Second, it declares that they should be a mutual help and comfort to one another. Finally, it is a framework within which they might have children. Adrian Thatcher argues that the first two of these reasons for marriage can quite easily be applied to same-sex couples seeking the blessing of the Church.[7] The voices of the couples have already revealed a wish to be seen as open in relationship within their families and within the wider society. This is because they wish to develop a lifestyle of security and faithfulness that such a framework would enable them to enjoy. They recognise security and faithfulness as a healthy and holistic ways of living and feel let down by social structures that do not accommodate them by not recognising them.

127

> All that we have done is a proper marriage as far as our friends and family are concerned and as far as we feel. Furthermore, I think that it is the way that we are regarded by God because of the way we have made our commitment to each other. The only area that I have a problem with is the law. We are not accepted. As an example, yesterday I was making a phone call with regard to a pension scheme and because we are not legally married, in the event of my death, no pension will be payable to Paul. *(Chris, Couple 4)*

All couples had experience of discrimination under the law that they wanted to see remedied. All were emphatic that the law should change to allow them the same rights as their heterosexual counterparts. What became clear was that a ceremony in Church was not only something that gave credence to who they were as a couple in a recognised public forum, but it was a place in which their voices could be heard.

> Marriage for lesbian and gay couples should exist especially from a legal point of view. There are still certain advantages that heterosexual couples can have that we cannot have in law, particularly in the event of one of us dying. Financial means don't automatically go to your same-sex partner unless you make a will. There are all sorts of things that Ruth would not receive if I died – like my pension, just because we are not legally married. *(Amelia, Couple 2)*

> And really just crazy silly things, like paternity leave. Amelia has just had a baby. If you are in a same-sex relationship you are not able to have paternity leave because you are not the one who has had a baby. You are not a father and so you are not entitled to paternity leave. I don't see why we shouldn't be the same as anyone else in that sense. We committed ourselves to a mortgage, we have committed ourselves to each other. I would like the law to be fair.
> *(Ruth, Couple 2)*

We do the same things as heterosexual couples. We pay the bills together, we pay the same taxes as them. Nearly everything is exactly the same apart from the fact that we are not allowed to get married. It happens in Holland and Denmark . . . so if they can think about lowering the age of consent why can't they think about allowing us the responsibility of getting married? *(Karen, Couple 3)*

I think that whatever it is, it should have the same legal rights. If I die, Ian will not get my pension and vice versa. There should be some recognition for gay couples as there is for heterosexuals in that context. *(Steve, Couple 5)*

Marriage for gays and lesbians should be allowed, definitely, without a shadow of a doubt. There are some people who still don't want to recognise us as a couple even though we have been through a church service. It comes down to things like wills and next of kin. *(Douglas, Couple 6)*

The voices of the discriminated might well be the voices of the biblical 'poor'. Yet for all the fuss inside the Church surrounding the acceptance and affirmation of gay and lesbian couples, scant attention has been accorded to the elemental human rights described by the 'voices' recorded here. On the contrary there are some that deny that they are authentic discriminations at all and that it is inappropriate that the Church should heed them.

What is this oppression, this wrong, this injustice? If it is that they are being despised and rejected by sections of society on account of their sexual inclination, are in fact victims of homophobia, then indeed they have a grievance which must be redressed . . . If on the other hand the 'wrong' or 'injustice' complained of is society's refusal to recognise homosexual partnerships as a legitimate alternative to heterosexual marriages, then talk of 'justice' is inappropriate, since human beings may not claim as a right what God has not given them.[8]

Discrimination does not occur in the abstract. Many gay people travelling to work, attending a business lunch, visiting someone in hospital or doing a thousand other things will be indistinguishable from most heterosexual people. It is in the real world that discrimination occurs. It is the visible partnership, the open relationship that reveals sexual orientation and risks rejection. Furthermore, in declaring what God gives to whom, one is left asking the question of just who decides that? It would seem that those who pronounce gay marriage to be an undermining of heterosexual marriage and a threat to traditional family values might also be those most nervous of losing control over what can and cannot happen.

There was little to be found in the conversation with the couples that even hinted that the blessing of same-gender partnerships would constitute an undermining of the institution of marriage or destabilise the values of what it means to live as a family. On the contrary, most felt that their wish for marriage or something like it was a testimony to the respect that they accorded it.

> I don't think that I want to undermine marriage. What we have is just love and I think that churches should open their doors to that other kind of love. It enriches rather than undermines.   *(Daniela, Couple 1)*

> I don't see how it can undermine marriage. I think that it can only make it get stronger, because it enforces the fact that love is best bonded in committed relationship. You want the best for your partner and any children you might care for. How can that be undermining anything?   *(Anna, Couple 3)*

> I think in a way it probably underpins marriage because it is to say that having a blessing is an unconventional form of marriage. As far as family is concerned it needs to be remembered that lots of gay people are still part of families. So I don't think that being gay or having a blessing under-

mines it. Sometimes in strong families it may actually enhance it.   *(Ian, Couple 5)*

When you undermine something, you put it down. What have I got to gain from that? Douglas and I have nothing to gain in our present circumstances. Even though we are faithful we are not recognised. When I die any of my family could contest my will and take all this stuff in this flat which we bought together. Gay couples have to marry for love as things stand now. There is no other security for us. So how do I undermine marriage?   *(Stephen, Couple 6)*

In defining a same-gender partnership as a prospective marriage there may be some debate around the nurture of children. While it is impossible for same-gender couples to procreate with each other, some do opt to raise children either by adoption or through artificial insemination. In his early (already cited) book *Liberating Sex*, Adrian Thatcher argues that the inability to have children of one's own is never considered a good reason to invalidate the marital integrity of opposite-sex couples in marriage. This being so, why then should it be introduced as an argument of conviction to deny same-sex couples the same status? However in a later work, *Marriage after Modernity*,[9] he recognises procreation as a critical feature of heterosexual marriage as defined in history. It is this critical feature that has made marriage a heterosexual institution, and for some gay and lesbian couples an institution that has marginalised them. This has come about because the effect of marriage has been seen to declare itself as the only way that Christians in particular and all others generally ought to relate sexually.[10] However, he notes that marriage has endured a degree of reshaping over the years. The purposes of marriage outlined in the *Book of Common Prayer* of 1662 are altered or re-arranged in the revised *Alternative Services Book* of 1980 and *Common Worship* of 2000. The purpose of marriage is no longer seen as the avoidance of fornication. Instead, the principal purpose of marriage is so that the couple may minister to each other. This is followed by the recognition that they are to live openly in the community. Finally it is that they might have the gift and care of children. Thatcher notes that numerous gay and lesbian couples, unable to procreate with each other, still enjoy the gift and care of children. These are their responsibility either because one or other or both of the partners had been previously in a union producing children with someone of the opposite sex, or by adoption, or by artificial insemination. Of the six couples taking part in this research, three had children by a marriage (one had grandchildren), one couple had a child by artificial insemination and one couple were pursuing a process for adoption. Thatcher poses the question, should the inability to procreate be sufficient reason to prevent gay and lesbian couples who so wish, to be married? He goes on to offer two alternatives. The first is to view marriage as a heterosexual institution because of the historic link with procreation. The second is to say that the theology of marriage can be extended to same-gender couples.[11]

While there are some who question the *translation* of heterosexual marriage to incorporate gay and lesbian relationships there are others (including many gay and lesbian people) who question the *desirability* of such an option. There seems to be no single answer. Elizabeth Stuart asserts that with one in three marriages failing, marriage itself is in trouble. What good reason is there then to recommend it to gay and lesbian couples?[12] Marriage as an institution has a poor track record for many women in particular. She opts for a model of friendship as one that is most fulfilling, particularly for women couples.

What was clear in my conversation with the couples was that this model of friendship as a way of being in relationship was one that they almost all valued. Some of the women had been in (what appeared to be) abusive relationships with men. Some of the men had also had poor experiences in previous relationships that had scarred them, and healing had taken time. The element of friendship was one that they had cultivated during the period of getting to know one another and was central to the relationship.

> For me it is almost as if this is more than a marriage. When we are together we do things together. We share things. Yes, and when she has to go I feel like as we say in Italian, 'half an orange'. Then I need to phone her and to hear her voice. I want to talk to her. I need to talk to her. It's the only person who I feel like that. Not with my children, nor with another friend, but with her, yes.   *(Christina, Couple 1)*

If gay and lesbian couples were not looking for marriage then there were some that indicated that they were certainly looking for something very like it. This would support Thatcher's theory that the theology of marriage might be extended to couples of the same sex without dislocating it from its historical evolution. For some like Paul, what he has experienced in preparing for a ceremony of blessing and covenanted union is so close to what he has seen of marriage ceremonial that it is indistinguishable. That his partner is not female is of no significance in this instance.

> I see it as a marriage because it was blessed in front of other people. I see a marriage as a bond between two loving people – not necessarily a man and a woman. I don't think that we should be treated any differently.   *(Paul, Couple 4)*

Whether such relationships are better described in a language that is not formed from a thousand years of heterosexual Christian marriage has yet to be ascertained. There were some that would like to avail themselves of a change in the law that would lift the current discrimination against them.

> I would like to be married and it would be marvellous if everyone would recognise us because I think that gay people are treated differently from straight people.   *(Steve, Couple 5)*

> So, yes, I consider myself to be married but if they legalised marriage (for gay people) tomorrow I would do the service again so that it could be legalised.   *(Chris, Couple 4)*

Amongst members of the church community there were those

who likewise hoped for a time when at the very least the option for marriage would be made available to gay and lesbian couples.

> . . . blessing would mean a great deal to the couple, I should think. They would give a great deal of thought to it; perhaps even more than young couples who were entering marriage because it is quite a statement to make I think. To talk about it as a marriage gets us into legalities here. I suppose the time will come when there will be a form of marriage for homosexual people. It might be too early for people to accept but I can't really see anything wrong with it.   *(June, C2)*

Others similarly recognised that there is more at stake for same-gender couples wanting recognition of their union than for opposite-sex couples seeking marriage. They have to look harder than opposite-sex couples for a community and place that will accept them and endorse their union.

> I think that such a service would mean much the same as for a man and a woman in marriage, maybe more because they have had to overcome more hurdles. I would like to think that it means just as much or they wouldn't go through with it.   *(Moira, C2)*

This view merely confirmed the experience of such couples looking for a place of welcome, safety and liberty, as already described by their own voices.

Blessing and the language of covenant and commitment
Within the church community, most of those who took part from all sections of the church seemed clear as to what a blessing of gay and lesbian couples was *not*. Although many of them saw it as analogous to marriage as they knew it (a heterosexual institution) for most of them it was not the same as a marriage. Like some of the couples a number wished for something distinct from marriage but with the same status and legal securities. Others wished for marriage to be made an option for those who wanted it. Still others

saw value in the act of blessing as distinct from these options. All continued to struggle to find a precise alternative language with which to describe the pastoral practice of their local church that they were able to support. Various descriptive themes emerged in this period of the reflective process, all of which made a contribution to defining what they thought occurred in an act of blessing. Some church members saw it as a sign revealing *commitment* and *mutuality* as the predominant themes.

> When the couple ask for God's blessing, it is upon their commitment to each other for the rest of their lives. That is where the blessing focuses for me. This step is one that changes their outlook on the way they intend to live the rest of their lives. *(Millie, C1)*

> It is something for a solid relationship. It is not something to be done for the sake of publicity. *(Doreen, C1)*

> God makes a statement in blessing. In that partnership and its blessing the two people are committing themselves in faithfulness to one another. I would like to think that it is giving them a bit more stability. *(Lavinia, C1)*

> A blessing is a way of showing that they are committing themselves to each other to stay together. I suppose that they are asking God's blessing on this intention. A blessing is different from a marriage but I think it is a kind of sealing of their commitment. It must represent something in their relationship and to everyone else as well. It is a public commitment and a commitment to God too, which may be why they have chosen it to take place in church. *(Daisy, C3)*

The senior members felt that a service of blessing made a difference to the lives of the couples, something that the couples themselves had already expressed. Other church members too thought that it made a distinct change to the life of the couple, while still more felt that the difference was to be located as much in the members of the local church community themselves as in the couples. For those that could remember them, some members of the congregation noticed a change of view towards Rodney and Saxon as a result of sharing in their anniversary service in 1985. One person made reference to the service of memorial held at St Luke's following Rodney's death in 1995. Ten years after their 'silver jubilee' people had turned out in great numbers for that service of memorial, and Jennifer was convinced it was a mark of their affirmation for and recognition of Saxon as Rodney's surviving partner as much as for Rodney himself.

> I was amazed at how many people came to the service for Rodney after he died. I was there that night. I was amazed. The church was packed. I thought well, it just shows you, people are not all against it.   *(Jennifer, C1)*

Daisy (quoted above) identifies the act of blessing as having three distinct areas of commitment. It is firstly a sign of commitment from the couple to each other. It is secondly a sign of commitment between the couple to the community of faith, family and friends, and finally it is a sign of their commitment to God. This threefold vision of commitment perhaps emphasises most strongly the relational value of blessing. One of the gifts of blessing would appear to be the sense in which it brings the relationship into the open.

> The blessing on my partnership with Ian is one that now sees us recognised as a couple in the eyes of God. Also, making the vows before God leaves me feeling more aware now that I have made a very serious commitment. To break it would demand a lot of forgiveness from everyone who attended the ceremony and especially Ian.   *(Steve, Couple 5)*

Couples, who have hitherto found they live so discretely as to be almost secretive about who they are and how they are as a couple, are enabled, by this sign to declare publicly in a safe environment their commitment to life partnership. That this is reflected further in the commitment that the gathered community makes to them extends the desire for openness. This is a symbol of considerable importance in covenant theology. God's relationship with Israel that is renewed time and again in the establishment and re-establishment of the first covenant is similarly depicted as open and in the 'light' through the establishment of God's second covenant in the person of Jesus Christ.

If we can see the need for openness in this way and find it reflected in Judaic/Christian covenant theology, then it raises for all engaged in pastoral ministry and parish life a related issue. Can a service of blessing (or any service for that matter) be done privately? There is strong pressure from different parts of the Church at this time either to behave in a reactive and sometimes reactionary way to those that disagree with their view on so affirming gay and lesbian relationships, or to go underground. I am not inclined to encourage a pursuit of either path. None of those interviewed from the church community saw that the activity of blessing same-gender partnerships was part of a conspiracy or campaign to see a particular point of view prevail. Some were quite clear that such a move would be counter-productive. All were aware that in the current climate there was still the risk of misrepresentation and that even acting with the fullest integrity, the possibility of confrontation might still occur. Thus there was a disinclination to 'advertise' any more than one would advertise any other aspect of ministry or liturgical service offered in a parish church.

One member of the congregation thought that in the current climate, discretion might mean that St Luke's should lean towards the private ceremony as the preferred option.

> If two individuals want to do this and it is okay with the rector, then it needs to be talked through, however I don't think it is something that the Church should be promoting at this stage. *(Roger, C3)*

Sometimes this is also the expectation of the couples.

> I was surprised at how much there was involved in a cere-
> mony like this. When we came to see you, I simply thought
> that you would take us over to the church and do a simple
> ceremony of blessing there and then in front of the altar.
> *(Ian, Couple 5)*

Such a style of operating was the standard form in the Church for a long time. In 1981 I remember taking part in my first ceremony of covenanted union for a lesbian couple. The two women were regular members of the church congregation. They had been together for a number of years, always attended church together and are now, 20 years later, still in faithful partnership. Their ceremony lasted between three and five minutes one Sunday morning after the Parish Eucharist. They appeared at the side chapel while the rest of the congregation was having a cup of coffee after the morning worship. The vicar did the prayers and I carried the rings from the altar to the couple. They exchanged the rings, embraced and went to coffee. Most people, even in the church community, were oblivious of the ceremony, and yet most knew that the two women were together. Openness can bring a degree of risk, but silence and secrecy have far more damaging consequences in the long term for a Church that seeks wholeness. Historically, those members of St Luke's who can remember know that some public ceremony in the domain of same-gender blessings attracted negative attention in the past. Following adverse press coverage on the twenty-fifth anniversary for Saxon and Rodney in 1985, further services for other couples were relocated to the small chapel at the St Richard's church centre. This is a small mission church building in another part of the parish of Charlton. Most of the 32 blessing services that took place until 1994 were held there. Congregations tended to be smaller and the proceedings carried a greater degree of informality. However, they remained open services. If an understanding of blessing is that it is something that is open then a commitment to the integrity of that ethos requires careful overseeing. By 1995, all services of blessing were again taking place in the parish church.

If blessing was perceived by the church community as a demonstration of God's commitment to the couple because of their commitment to each other and the commitment of the faith community to participate and support it, then blessing was also a foundation for stability. The church community saw it as an important feature to provide an opportunity for stability within the wider community. In the case of individuals or 'minority' groups with a particular sense of feeling unsupported or even persecuted, it was all the more important to affirm stability and commitment in the partnerships they were undertaking.

> . . . a public . . . affirmation of what they stand for and how they love one another and want that relationship recognised and blessed can only be something which will give them the stability and, I suppose, the sense of total commitment. *(Lavinia, C1)*

Recognition seemed to be a theme that linked quite naturally to the concept of affirmation. The public nature of the blessing enables the couple to be 'seen' or recognised as a couple. If blessing is a way of bringing something into the light then it enables couples to be 'recognised' as such, at least by their friends and family.

Commitment and stability were obvious features that couples were looking for in entering a process of preparing for a service of covenant and blessing. For most this was bound by the degree of acceptance they found both within the local church and what they perceived of God through their encounter with the local church.

> Being blessed by God through the Church feels to me like an act of acceptance. So what it means is that it feels like I am accepted within however small a proportion of the Church. As far as I am concerned God was present in that ceremony and God says it's okay. *(Ruth, Couple 2)*

> I feel that it is an acceptance from a Church that for a lot of years has not accepted gay people in this way. I see the

blessing as an acceptance from God that our relationship is not abnormal. For this reason it meant so much to find God's blessing in a church. It was like the Church's blessing for us is God's blessing. *(Anna, Couple 3)*

For some this acceptance was particularly healing in that it directly addressed the wounds of destructive rejections from the past. To be blessed by God means to be healed by God and to grow.

For me blessing meant that we were being accepted by the Church and that we were being accepted by God. This was particularly important because of the experience I'd had at the previous church where I had been shunned for leading a gay lifestyle. So it actually gave me some peace of mind to know that I was being accepted. *(Chris, Couple 4)*

Many recognised the strengthening power of blessing. Its value for them was not merely in the ceremony but in what they felt they took away from the ceremony into a new phase of life together. For Amelia this was not simply because it enabled her to feel accepted publicly, it was because by it God named what she was doing.

I feel similar to Ruth. It felt important and I have continued to feel blessed. It wasn't something that just happened at the ceremony and ended at the doors. It felt important to be blessed during the ceremony because it gave a name to being blessed by a higher being which we call God. *(Amelia, Couple 2)*

It's a blessing because it has given us more strength as a couple. It is not something that goes away, like you get blessed one day and that is it. The blessing, the strength stays with you. It helps that we can remember the ceremony because it is something that is often in your mind and that you think about. I think that the act of blessing stabilises the relationship and makes it stronger. *(Stephen, Couple 6)*

Members of the congregation were able to identify with these sentiments. Knowing that relationships need sustaining, they recognise the power of signs, symbols and ceremonial and the things they purport to convey.

> Perhaps the couples feel more united if they have a blessing. Wally and I do. That Pat Joseph who comes to our church, she wears a ring doesn't she? A lot of people do that when they get married. We didn't but I do know it is what happened for Pat and her partner. To some people, they think that gays and lesbians are odd compared to a normal man and wife, but then we must seem odd to them, mustn't we? So it goes two ways doesn't it?   *(Edna, C3)*

In preparation for a service of blessing and covenanted union the practice at St Luke's is to be very clear that no matter how much the ceremony may *seem* like a marriage in the hearts of the couple, it has no legal status. While this means that in the unfortunate event of a breakdown in the relationship couples are spared the misfortune of the divorce courts, it is, therefore, as already described, a more precarious union to enter into. Earlier in this chapter Stephen laments the lack of status for his partner and knows that he leans on the good will of his family if his poor health breaks down completely and he dies. In January 2000 this is exactly what happened and a very moving funeral service took place for him in the parish church where he and Douglas had made, and annually renewed, their vows of faithfulness to each other. Douglas was well supported by Stephen's family, but was not allowed to register the death as next of kin. Similarly, in his dealings with the funeral directors, though present he could not be recorded as the next of kin. It was only at the funeral itself that his position as the one that had faithfully cared for his partner could be accorded the honour it was due. Because of the lack of legal status and security, all couples are invited to demonstrate their material care for each other by preparing in advance a last will and testament that is then signed in lieu of marriage registers during the course of the ceremony. None of the couples are obliged to do this, but all taking part in this book chose to.

The significance of this legal insecurity has already been described. The effect that it has on most couples is to encourage them in their disadvantaged position to work even harder at their relationship and how they describe it publicly. For most it heightens the moral standing they choose to give it.

> For me, being blessed in church is a sort of ethical thing. We are making a commitment and we are trying to give every effort to live out and fulfil that commitment. *(Ian, Couple 5)*

> Being blessed meant that I felt that I was giving myself fully to Stephen and not just for the sake of it. Having the blessing meant that I understood this to be something that was from God. *(Douglas, Couple 6)*

It was clear to most of the couples that what they were embarking on was a venture with no legal authority, but a high level of moral integrity. Although none argued that a moral authority defined their service of blessing, most saw it as an expression of moral value.

> Being blessed was like it was God's agreement on what we were trying to do. God, to me, has always been presented as love and we love each other so we are actually doing what God wants. *(Paul, Couple 4)*

Paul, who has grown up entirely untouched by a formal church upbringing, defines an image of God that is drawn from Scripture and through which he feels able to describe the honesty of his feelings as the model for his partnership. God is love and so when Paul feels love for Chris, he feels that he enters into God's love. It is not only because God loves, but also because God *is* love that this is able to happen at all. This Paul describes as 'doing what God wants'.

Many of the church members thought that the subject of whether a service of blessing had any moral authority was one that concerned personal sexual morality. Arthur (C2) thought that services of blessing merely fed a neurosis that gay and lesbian couples were susceptible to, although he thought that heterosexual couples getting married felt that way too. Mary (C2) had a high sense of moral authority which while located in God was dispensed through the church. James (C1) saw it not so much as a sign of moral authority but rather as a sign of changing of times. Sara (C3) saw it as moral in the sense that it provided a challenge to the human legal institution of Law.

> Yes, a blessing has moral authority in that it is a personal commitment. I think that the things about the legal authority are being challenged all the time.   *(Sara, C3)*

Interestingly these were perspectives of moral authority that covered different areas from those prioritised by the couples. Other members of the church community however defined the question of blessing as one in which morality and authority met in partnership. When this approach was taken they saw the Church as a vehicle of God's blessing and therefore a model of authority. Perhaps it is in exercising a perceived moral authority that the Church can make a difference.

> I don't know if it (blessing) would make a change (to the couple). I suppose it must in the same way as marriage makes a change. Even people who have lived together for a long time or in a permanent way before they are married feel different after the marriage. I think that this public commitment asking for God's blessing and the fact that a priest representing God's blessing has been there and performed that function must mean that you feel you can go forward positively with this permanent union.   *(Mary, C2)*

In rather different language the youth of St Luke's state something similar.

> A blessing is a kind of way in which God shows approval.

143

> So it is a kind of acknowledgement that these two are a couple and they want to be together. It's like God giving a blessing through the Church. They make a commitment and then God sends love onto the couple. It sort of wishes them success on their relationship. *(Tom, C5)*

Seen this way the act of 'blessing' becomes something that meets the positive human statement of faithfulness with a positive theological response of faithfulness. God's blessing, conveyed through the Church, is one that not only endorses the couple but also contributes to their growing in maturity as a couple – as it might of any couple. That has to be a good thing.

> It takes place in church. You can't go to a registry office and have a blessing. It is a commitment to God. *(Daisy, C3)*

While the preoccupation with an act of blessing might lie in the preparation for life together, it would be churlish to play down the significance of the 'big day' itself. Few would dispute that the commitment to a faithful partnership is an important milestone in life. The marking of such an occasion defines the partnership and the changed way of life to be adopted. Couples and local church-members alike recognised blessing as instrumental in that change.

> The act of blessing was something that I felt within, but outwardly it gave a name to a process. It is very hard to describe. *(Amelia, Couple 2)*

> If you have a reason to celebrate, then it gives a date and a place. *(Sara, C3)*

A time and a place mark the very act of blessing, as for many other rites of passage. This is significant. Just as married couples often return to the place where they made their vows of commitment and some like to renew them, there is something intrinsic in the nature of blessing that draws encouragement from being able to reflect upon beginnings or major life changes. There is strong scriptural support for such a view of blessing. Jacob's metaphorical wrestling with God at Peniel[13] might be cited as a new era in his life story that was marked with the demand for a blessing. In other passages, particularly within the Pentateuch, places of blessing were marked with the building of an altar or some other sign of the sacred. Two of the couples mark the anniversary of their ceremony of covenanted union with a brief service of renewal each year. Most of the others visit at other times. All are invited to special festivals as are those who have been married in the course of the year or had children baptised.

Whatever else blessing means to either the couples who seek ministry from the Church or those in the local church community who support their search, an act of enabling seems to take place. A church community that holds a vision of empowerment as an essential way of being 'church' discovers this in the gift of empowerment itself. Couples, marginalised in many quarters of Church and Society, during a period of preparation to receive authorised blessing are encouraged to take responsibility for the outcome of a ceremony that will describe their commitment to each other. While there is little doubt that this challenges a stereotypical view of gay and lesbian relationships and, within Church and Society poses a challenge to their validity, these are secondary features in this pastoral practice. The primary features lie in the capacity for a local church to respond to the needs of a small but significant group in the local neighbourhood. A couple wants their relationship affirmed and the opportunity to declare publicly their commitment to each other. With no legal apparatus to support them, they approach the local church. The local church sees this as an opportunity to live out its identity through its ministry. It becomes a place of welcome, it provides sanctuary for the marginalised couple and it creates the space in which they can be empowered. This is the perceived blessing.

> There is significance in saying we love each other and we want to tell the world . . . Laws are changing all the time.

> People are taking their cases to the court of human rights.
> So, eventually we will see.   *(Sara, C3)*

Amongst the church members a significant proportion revealed their support for the practice of blessing same-gender couples (72 per cent) and as will be seen in the next chapter, this same proportion were keen that this ministry should continue. Many saw the practice of blessing couples as going some way to redressing the unequal status of same-gender couples who wanted to make public commitment to sharing lifelong partnerships.

> It's like, if heterosexuals can get married then why can't
> we?   *(Sara, C3)*

> I should imagine that for those people (the couples) they
> realise that the world we live in is grossly unfair and that
> this is the nearest they are going to get (to a marriage).
> *(Sally, C2)*

> I would regard it as something that does what a conventional
> marriage ceremony does.   *(Mary, C2)*

> In a sense it is like a kind of marriage.   *(Eddy, C5)*

Similarly, as we have seen, many of the couples expressed the same kind of feelings. Most simply wanted the same opportunity as the greater proportion of responsible citizens to declare publicly their love for another person and make vows of commitment to them.

> I thought it was the proper thing to do within the eyes of
> God and it was showing our friends that we were making a
> real commitment and not just going to live together.   *(Paul,
> Couple 4)*

Although the support for services of blessing was not unanimous, there was an indication throughout the congregational reflection that the practice of blessing was justified because it went some way to directly addressing the perception of one congregation that gay and lesbian couples are discriminated against. That being so, if the language of blessing is the language of light as indicated earlier then it is brought to bear on a shadowy situation where same-gender couples are kept quiet and hidden in parts of both Church and Society. Thus the language of blessing becomes a language of liberation, a language that announces God's justice through the pastoral action of the Church. For some church members, being brought to the light is perceived as an encounter with liberty. The activity of blessing same-sex couples is then seen to be a blessing because it highlights the injustice of their situation and calls for change. However, there always exists a tension between the commitment to openness in public ceremony and the risk of merely utilising pastoral liturgy of this kind as a campaigning technique.

If the language of blessing can be expressed in the language of liberty then it presents us with a model of God as generosity. God is generous in the dispensing of grace and that means that we need to take seriously an understanding expressed by some gay and lesbian couples (as Paul earlier) that it is through their love for and commitment to each other that they find and express the love of God. This is important as it brings us face to face with the possibility that God might grace a type of relationship and a way of living that is currently not sanctioned officially by the Church. What this means for the Church is that the self-perception that it is the vehicle of God's grace is challenged by a wider perception that God is not restricted to the body of the Church as a means of dispensing that grace. Of the couples, Daniela noted that in her experience the Church sometimes seemed to appear as an obstacle to God's grace. However, for God that was not as significant a problem as it might be for the Church.

> It is very difficult for me to answer what it means to be blessed. Maybe it only confirms what I thought before. I think that there is only one God, but sometimes the Church's ideas are crooked you know. They don't get round to the

> point, but it is different with God. Now I have come to
> the conclusion that there is nothing wrong with our relation-
> ship, and besides, the Church is not the only way God
> works. *(Daniela, Couple 1)*

In this perception we are introduced to the theological idea that
the whole of creation is graced. What we look for are signs of
that grace. Adrian Thatcher suggests that one such sign in gay and
lesbian partnerships is that of what he calls 'mutuality in ministry'.

> . . . Connections may be made between heterosexual and
> homosexual partnerships with regard to the sacramentality
> of each . . . The sacramental understanding expressed in
> this book deliberately adopted the term 'communal partner-
> ship' as the 'matrix' of the sacrament. Indeed 'mutuality in
> ministry' is more likely, in fact, to be expressed in avowed
> egalitarian relationships than in hierarchical ones (as mar-
> riage has been for most of its history).[14]

He goes on to support this by appealing to the theology of
Karl Rahner and in particular his famous essay 'Marriage as a
Sacrament'.[15] In brief, Rahner espoused the view that the whole of
creation was graced by the love of the creator. That it was created
at all was an act of love. Consequently, if God is the source of that
love then the signs of that love are found in the evidence of creation
and in the love expressed in human relationships. What marks out
God's love as generous is the way that it challenges human love
when it sets limits for itself. God's love is limitless. For Rahner
there is no distinction between the commandment to love God and
the commandment to love one's neighbour. Loving our neighbour
is the means by which we express love for God. It follows then,
that all personal relationships are the signs of our relationship with
God.

If the sacramental grace of God is something that is available to
all because it is so generously dispensed as to allow us the potential
to find God in all things, then it follows that it is not confined to
the heterosexual relationship and the institution of heterosexual

marriage. Seen like this, God's grace is a means of empowerment to the couples who feel hidden and unwanted, and a gift to the Church that is confined by the limits of its own capacity to love, in the light of God's love.

> God is not so illiberal. The commitments of lesbian and gay people in their partnerships are no less sacramental, no less able to be a 'sign' of that divine love which is Jesus Christ.[16]

The model of God as a generous dispenser of loving grace is one that enables individual Christians and church communities to grow by extending the boundary limits of their own love in the pursuit of limitless love. If this model can be applied to the local church community of St Luke's and its reflection on 20 years of supporting lesbian and gay couples, then it highlights significant change within that community. Church members noted that this change began during the time that Saxon and Rodney lived amongst them. From that time when Saxon and Rodney came to St Luke's in November 1978 for their service of blessing to the occasion of their twenty-fifth anniversary in 1985, there was a shift in consciousness within the congregation at St Luke's. In a magazine interview Saxon and Rodney noted the change.

> When their marriage was first blessed at St Luke's, where they were both parish councillors, there was an open invitation to the parish. Five people turned up. Six years later in May 1985, when they renewed their vows to celebrate their 25th anniversary, 150 people joined the ceremony. They see this as how people's attitudes can be changed, from inside the community rather than from its fringe.[17]

If the risk of celebrating this partnership through a service of covenanted union was deemed a worthy one in 1979 then it is clear that the exercising of that liberty was one that brought much blessing to a church community in subsequent years. It was deemed to be a gesture of generosity given by the church community that eventually came back to them. However, the act of generosity was one that led to some conflict. The larger congregation that assembled in 1985 for the twenty-fifth anniversary was met by a small group of Christian fundamentalist protesters. The national tabloid-press reported the story and in so doing sensationalised and ultimately trivialised the event and its implications.

> One barged past the white robed men, stormed the pulpit . . . condemning homosexuality as a sin . . . a second demonstrator disrupted prayers, begging God not to destroy the church after the 'blasphemous' service.[18]

In the short term this level of reporting merely revealed a gulf in the thinking and attitude between the local church community whose story and experience were being told, and those for whom the press were writing. In the long term it has provided a clear benchmark defining the degree of societal change that has occurred in that time. What was clear then, and is now, is that even when a blessing is given in the spirit of generosity so as to be liberating, it will sometimes be a catalyst for confrontation with those who lead the Church and those who most influence its thinking and teaching. As we will see later, from the days of the Jesus movement, it was ever thus.

CHAPTER 6

Voices Begging to Differ

what does it mean to be doing the christian thing?

Chapters Four and Five have endeavoured to give an empathetic hearing to the voices of a church community and some of those who are met in that community's ministry of support and affirmation. It is likely that some will see this as a laudable action, but critics will rightly ask what is distinctly Christian about it? What is it that justifies the gift of blessing to a relational lifestyle that is not generally regarded as the 'norm' in society and is not reflected either in Scripture or in the inherited traditions of the Church?

These questions and the issues raised by the voices in this reflection will not be properly answered until the question of what we think God is doing in and for the world has first been addressed. In an essay entitled 'But isn't "It" a Sin?'[1] Mark Taylor borrows a phrase from G. K. Chesterton to address this question. Chesterton speaks of 'doing the Christian thing' and Taylor asks what precisely it means to be 'doing the Christian thing'. What is the heart of the Christian message and existence all about? If this question can be addressed then we may be in a position to pose a further question and look at whether faithful same-sex partnerships violate what God does in Jesus in the world. In this chapter I will begin to explore what the 'voices' of the church community understand by the Christian thing and whether they see the pastoral practice of supporting lesbian and gay couples and blessing their unions in the name of God as a violation of that Christian thing. The chapter will necessarily focus principally upon these voices, but it will offer the voices of the couples the chance to corroborate or contradict these perceptions as they reflect upon the influence of their encounter with the local church and their experience of its ministry.

At the beginning of their reflection the voices of the church community revealed a degree of uncertainty as to what the status and practice of blessing gay and lesbian couples at St Luke's was and the frequency with which it occurred. Chapter Four showed that while some like Millie had first-hand experience of assisting at services of covenant and blessing, others like Lavinia knew that it was a part of the church's past. She wonders whether the casual visitor would know whether it was a feature of life in the present. At this point in the reflection process it is made clear that the church practice *is* one in which same-sex couples are supported through services of covenanted union and blessing. The church members then began to consider whether this is a practice that could be regarded as reflecting the ethos of Christian life.

Overall 72 per cent of those who took part thought it was in keeping with a Christian view of life, 16 per cent thought it not and 12 per cent were undecided. Many thought that living the Christian life was seen to place the individual follower of Christ in a precarious position from time to time, and it was the young people of the church who drew on their experiences of prejudice to respond to this question. They saw church as a place of sanctuary for all sorts and conditions of people and drew on a strong awareness of anti gay and lesbian attitudes at large. As a kind of sexism they were able to categorise it in the same league as they would racial discrimination. It was important for them that gay and lesbian people should be allowed to feel safe both within the Church and outside it. Some of them had first-hand experience of friends who had been the victims of discrimination either because they were gay or black. Their appeal to experience was a very strong one as was their desire to resist discrimination and be clear that this was where they stood as part of the church community.

If people have anything against the way we do things, we should say that this is the way we do things and this is what we believe. If you don't believe this then that is fine, that is your choice. We are not asking anyone to become a part of this, but if they do feel similar then that is okay too. *(Emily, C5)*

The young members of the church thought that to support gay and lesbian people was a critical feature of church community life. For them it could best come about by enabling positive experiences within the community. Openness and the opportunity to educate through encounter were, in their view, the most creative ways forward.

The reason why there is so much difference [of opinion] is because there is not enough education. People often form their views out of ignorance. Instead of leaving everyone to their own devices I think that you should take the opportunity to introduce them to gay people. *(Nicola, C5)*

Amongst those in need of this educational experience, the youth perceived resistance to the acceptance of gay and lesbian partnerships as most likely to come from the elderly members of the congregation. Born in a generation when sex and relationships were not openly discussed, they saw the elderly as repressed and conservative in their attitudes.

We have got a lot of older members in the church and I think that in their day homosexuality was brushed under the carpet. I think that you start educating in church now because they are the ones who are going to hold the negative view because they are not used to it. *(Tom, C5)*

Ironically, the only other category of church member to be 100 per cent supportive of the church action to support and bless same-gender partnerships *was* the senior members. Far from brushing anything under the carpet, these all drew not on contemporary experiences of sexual prejudice, but on their 20-year long memories

153

of Rodney and Saxon. By way of contrast the language used by this category to describe what it meant to be 'doing the Christian thing' was not one of open resistance (as was the language of the youth) but one borne out of a desire to promote harmony and encourage sincerity.

> I think that this is in keeping with my view of the Christian life. Provided the people are sincere and it is what they want to do. When a marriage takes place, it is a sign that they have declared in front of people that they intend to live together in harmony and comfort to each other. I would say that a blessing has similar significance. As with marriage, which the Church sees as a right and proper thing, I would see the blessing of homosexual couples as a similar thing.
> (James, C1)

Lavinia described a church that over a period of years has come to a greater understanding of gay people. For her it was impossible to locate 'the Christian thing' or the Christian life in a single moment. It is something that is continually being unwrapped. The Rodney and Saxon event was an important one for the church community because it gave people at St Luke's the opportunity to experience and interact in the life of a same-gender couple to whom they could relate as people rather than dismiss as stereotype. Theologically this is an important point in that if the local church community is to see its life located in its encounter with the living Christ, then God will be revealed through the relationships that are formed in and around that community. Perhaps what Lavinia might be suggesting implicitly is that whether or not God is unchanging, what certainly does change are the perceptions we have of God. These perceptions are often informed by the perceptions we have of each other. They in turn inform the way we learn to relate to each other. What I think has taken place here is that an encounter in the life of the church community with a gay couple in 1978 has led them to a new way of experiencing what it means to be 'church' and to be 'doing the Christian thing'.

Two senior members adopted language that showed compassion

as central to their understanding of Christian life. Compassion for lesbian and gay people was perceived as important because of the 'they can't help the way they are made' factor. This is a phrase open to serious misrepresentation and so I want to spend some time with it and take note of it at two levels. The first is a generational level. When compared to the language deployed by the youngest voices this could quite easily be misunderstood as patronising rather than compassionate. 'We have to feel sorry for them – it is not their fault', almost implies that the homosexual make up is one with 'a piece missing'. An entire generation has looked at gay and lesbian relations as a minority way of life and therefore one to be dealt with in a number of ways. Many have demonised it, depicting gay men and lesbian women as promiscuous sexual predators. Others treated it as a mental abnormality that could be treated.[2] A positive view of Jennifer and Doreen's 'can't help it' factor would see it as genuinely compassionate rather than patronisingly tolerant.

Perhaps inadvertently they introduce us to the second level of response. It is one in which we enter into a state of alienation. The ability to alienate is one of the more sophisticated defence mechanisms of the human psyche. It is something that we are able to do in almost every area of human life. In his book on science fiction and religious themes, Mike Alsford illustrates this quite simply.[3] The term 'alien' means being that which is 'other' than someone or something else. In the world of science fiction, aliens have become a defining motif. Often their 'otherness' compared to human beings is characterised negatively. They are frequently depicted as ugly and frightening. They lack individual character. They terrorise and are invasive. They must be stopped at all costs because they somehow stand for a personification of evil. This is the way that many distance themselves from identifying with gay and lesbian people. Mary McCormick Maaga in her critical analysis of the tragedy that befell the Jonestown community in 1978 sees similar kinds of distancing with cults and sects that are perceived to be sufficiently different or other than mainstream denominations.[4]

> There is the tendency of any of 'us' to dehumanise 'them', in an effort to create a sense of self by excluding others. What would happen to our sense of 'self' as women, as religious practitioners, as seekers after social justice, as Americans if we integrated the 'them' of Jonestown into 'us'?[5]

Alsford tells us that the philosopher Hegel saw understanding alienation as central to understanding reality. For Hegel, the sense of self would not come about by the exclusion of all that is different or opposite from us. Instead, by encountering and overcoming that which alienates, each human being can come to a more authentic sense of self-being. He goes on to point out that when we do this we sometimes see that the things we fear in the 'other' are actually located in our sense of 'self'.

> Alien beings may reflect back at us, aspects of ourselves, things that we either admire or perhaps even fear in our own character. The notion of self-alienation has become common in Western understandings of human identity. Ever since the philosopher Hegel first deployed the term to explain how reality as a whole comes to an awareness of itself by overcoming its self-alienation, the idea that human being is in some sense fragmented-alienated from its true potential or by its dark side – has become a common place observation.[6]

Mary McCormick Maaga challenges those of us who would create the alien 'them' to address that part of the 'self' ('us') that needs to do this. What seems to have happened to the church community at St Luke's in 1978 was that at one important level this encounter with the 'other' took place. Since that time, the experience of knowing an openly gay couple has enabled a process of integration to happen. It is this experience that has brought them as a church community to where they are now. Nowadays for most people in the congregation, identifying members by sexual orientation is rather banal. The language of lesbian and gay as a means of stating what I am not and distancing me from what I perceive you to be is rapidly becoming obsolete in this community. Instead it is being replaced in a new generation of congregational awareness with a language that identifies members of the Christian community not by their sexual orientation but by the way that each tries to live the Christian life.

In trying to 'do the Christian thing' St Luke's is beginning to discover that it is engaged in the work of theology, but *how* is the work of theology to be done? Both Millie and Moira spoke of not knowing enough about theology to be able to argue for or against the blessing of same-sex couples. Both operate out of a received tradition that has always suggested that theology is the preserve of academics and the clergy because of its methodology. This is very undermining for the laity and leaves us with an unbalanced model of Church. If theology is seen as knowledge of God and that knowledge is held in one repository of the Church then it is a destabilising feature of that Church. In the local church community at St Luke's members who claimed to have insufficient 'theology' referred to that model. They then went on to describe a view of God that was informed by their experience and helped shape what they felt living the Christian life was all about.

> I don't know the theological arguments and I don't know enough about faith but I would be happy if St Luke's did this regularly.   *(Moira, C2)*

> When you say the Christian life then I find that I can accept it and then I wonder about the Bible and what that has to say. Not being a theologian, I wonder if I understand the Bible and being a true Christian. I just think that my God is a loving God . . . I should love people as they are . . . so yes it is in keeping with my views of the Christian life.   *(Millie, C1)*

Part of this experience then has been to discover that 'doing the Christian thing' is an integral part of what it means to be doing the work of theology. What I see at work in this Christian community is a desire to 'do the Christian thing' by locating it within the language of love and expressing it in egalitarian terms that are both inclusive and non-judgemental. This is taken up by June who adopts an expression that is closer to the resistance language of the young people than the compassion of those described earlier. For her 'all are equal before God'. This is not an uncommon phrase but it is particularly significant in that it roots itself in an ideology of the early Christian movement, reflected in Galatians 3:27. When the Galatian Christians meet as church there is no distinction between gender, race and class. To be *en christo* means to live within the Christian community as equals.

The language of love was central in Mary's interview. It is a perspective that has been adopted by a number of academic theologians. Daniel Migliore, who teaches at Princeton Theological Seminary, makes much of the term 'The Rule of Love'.[7] He commends it as a guiding principle for any discernment of same-sex relationships and the life of the Christian community. It was a not dissimilar recommendation to that of a working party commissioned by the General Assembly of the Presbyterian Church (USA) in 1988. This working party was asked to comment on the expression of human sexual nature in all kinds of work situations. Its conclusions were that all relations should be governed by an abiding principle of love and justice. Migliore argues that same-gender unions can be an appropriate expression of this rule of love and remain consistent with Scripture. He sees love, justice and fidelity as virtues that are mirrored in God. For him it is not a primary issue that the relationship is between two people of the same-sex, but whether that relationship is a mirror of the way God is revealed as relating in Christ to the world. His view is that '*Sola scriptura* cannot be isolated from *sola gracias* and *sola Christus*'. My view of St Luke's as a local church community reflecting on this issue is that the majority would concur.

That said, it is important to record that there were two dissenting voices amongst members of the congregation, each of whom gave a view that was opposed to the blessing of same-gender unions on the grounds that it was unbiblical. Both are emphatic that the word of Scripture seems to be the final word and neither allows for interpretation or the influences of reason, experience and the tradition of the Church.

> It is not in keeping with my view of the Christian life at all because as a Christian I go according to the Bible. What the Bible says is what I agree and I haven't seen anywhere in the Bible that same-sex couples are of God's making. God created the homosexual and the lesbian, but it doesn't say anywhere in the Bible that they should get together and live together as man and wife. *(Penny, C4)*

> You can use a lot of things in the Bible to prove no end of things, but to my satisfaction whilst homosexuality is far from new, it was always frowned upon. Therefore in my view, nothing has changed. It might be frowned upon but what goes on behind closed doors, goes on behind closed doors. *(Arthur, C2)*

This appeal to *sola scriptura* contrasts starkly with the view of the church's youth, who opted for a more open approach to biblical sources.

> If you are more flexible, you believe in what the Bible says and you think it is right partly with some things — because some things are a bit dodgy. Then you can have your own views mixed in with what the Bible says. The Bible, rather than being a kind of rulebook becomes a guide as to how you should live your life. *(Eddy, C5)*

For a Christian community grappling with any serious pastoral issue, the appeal to and use of canonical Scripture is very important. On the issue of same-gender relationships Scripture has very little to say and what St Luke's church community reveals at this point is that its membership reflects a variety of approaches to the responsible use of Scripture. The analysis of scriptural texts has been well documented by other writers[8] who arrive at various and often very different conclusions. I do not propose to spend time in this book in extensive scriptural analysis, for that has already been well done elsewhere. The reader looking for this will find some suggestions amongst the bibliographical material.

Members of the church community did raise concerns about the kind of society that we cultivate when we live together as a community. They declared that the cultural context that does not fully enable same-gender couples to live in open, faithful relationships is one that is likely to cultivate instead a climate of promiscuity and fleeting non-permanent sexual relationships.

> For me the blessing of gay and lesbian unions is in keeping with my view of the Christian life because I think that the most important thing is to follow the commandment of loving everybody. Promoting love — and I don't simply mean sex, has to be something that we should be doing. I think that the reason for so many of the difficulties that there have been with gays and lesbians and the apparent link with the development of AIDS is the issue of promiscuity. Promiscuity is a problem because we have been unable to see this as acceptable. Therefore, people with these feelings have had to have fleeting and non-permanent relationships. I don't think that this is right for anybody. So, to encourage commitment in love has to be right for the Church.   *(Mary, C2)*

This is a view that contrasts quite starkly with the views of Penny and Arthur who appeal to Scripture. For them, the options for life practices would be either to confine relational expression to the 'closed doors' that Arthur advocates, or accept the imposed celibacy that one must inevitably conclude from Penny's viewpoint. Both appear to offer a rather bleak prospect for healthy and honest living. The 'what goes on behind closed doors' option simply did not match the ethos of openness that the church community wanted to cultivate. Secrecy seemed to be the opposite of what they understood 'blessing' to be, namely a way of bringing things into the light. There were others who saw that the adoption of a celibate way of life might provide one answer, however it was noted that celibacy was a chosen way of life, not an imposed one.

It was to be seen as one that God called some people to. Other church members did not consider it to be the *only* alternative.

It may be that the cultural context is something that can be influenced at different levels. For Daisy (C3), 'doing the Christian thing' was not so much something that revealed itself in how each individual responded to having gay and lesbian couples come for blessing services, but in the general ethos of the church community. If a church community did not accept you on the grounds that you were in an active same-sex partnership, this might be an indication of the overall ethos of that community. Daisy felt it quite likely that such a lack of openness might leave a stranger open to feeling unwelcome for any one of a number of reasons, from wearing scruffy clothes to having noisy children.

This is a view of the Christian life that is synonymous with a new movement emerging in theological thinking called '*christo-praxis*'. One person has defined this as 'the acting and thinking that coalesce around lives of commitment to Christ'.[9] Recently members of my congregation presented me with a souvenir mug. On it were the letters WWJD? To their delight I had not a clue what they stood for and they gleefully educated me with the answer: What Would Jesus Do? The adoption of '*christopraxis*' as a Christian model might be simply summarised in this motif. For members of St Luke's the effectiveness of any community seeking to discern what it means to be 'doing the Christian thing' will be determined by the way in which it receives people and offers a ministry of hospitality and welcome. This is what they perceive the life of Jesus to be embracing. It is what they try to emulate as a community of 'lives of commitment to Christ', when they practise a ministry of hospitality and welcome. They stressed: a degree of openness that meant that no one would find themselves turned away *(Tina)*, the need to counter racial and sexual prejudice *(young people)*, opportunities to show support *(Daisy)* and a way of enabling people to feel that they can 'belong' if they want to *(Nathaniel)*. The desire to know Christ is one that reveals a congregation prepared to welcome with no conditions attached. For gay and lesbian couples seeking out the ministry of a local church for recognition and blessing this means standing against the repressive strains of discrimination towards sexual orientation, expression and lifestyle. Jesus the compassionate, non-violent resister of injustice is the model this church most desires to emulate, a model framed by a rule of love. For St Luke's church community 'doing the Christian thing' means embracing these features of discipleship.

> Our responsibilities as part of the Christian family go beyond the immediate family to the entire population as children of God. These are people who are just as valid as anyone else in the world. *(Nathaniel, C3)*

Adopting such a model of discipleship is of little use if it exists solely for the benefit of that church community. Church communities are committed to the care and nurture of those that are called to faith within them, but as already described, they also exist for the benefit of those who live outside them. There is little point in describing such an ethos of Christian living without it being reflected by those who meet the local church in the activity of its ministry.

Of the couples who shared their thoughts about same-gender blessing and how they perceived the Church, none found themselves describing St Luke's as a 'compassionate, non-violent resister of injustice'! However, what was clear as each couple told their story, was just how grateful they were to have found somewhere local within the wider institution of the Church that would listen seriously to them. In telling their story, most were able to offer some description of how they perceived the Church and how that had been shaped and changed by the experience of attending St Luke's. All were able to bear out the declaration of Nathaniel that a Church with a perception that it lives for the wider family of the human race is one that they can enter into. Furthermore several couples offered signs that their lives had been significantly changed and perhaps even graced by the encounter with the Church.

Daniela and Christina, who had long since given up on the Church, found that through their encounter with St Luke's they were able to find a meaningful way back in.

I have discovered the Church again through St Luke's.
(Daniela, Couple 1)

Most were simply glad to be received, accepted entirely as they were and not discriminated against because they were gay or lesbian living in an active, open partnership. They described meeting a church of welcome and acceptance.

> Lots of people think that gay couples can't be accepted in the Church. It is a generalisation. We found in going to St Luke's, just during our period of preparation, it was so warm and open. We attended the services and got to know some of the people. When we first arrived people said, 'You're the two . . . ah yes!' So I suppose we did stand out a bit, but that was okay. People were just so lovely to us.
> *(Amelia, Couple 2)*

> I feel more inclined to go to church now than I did before because I have been made to feel welcome. I just didn't know if I was going to be welcomed as a gay person and now that I have been I will be able to attend again. *(Anna, Couple 3)*

Some described a very human institution, a place where they could be met as people and offered the support that they were looking for. This was coupled with a perception that here was a place that valued faithfulness in partnership and that would enable them to find ways of doing that publicly.

> My view of the Church has changed with working through St Luke's. I was mentioning about being taken seriously and the presentation of a more human face in matters relating to sexual orientation and gender etc. One thing that came across was your commitment to us. I now feel that the Church has a place in my life. *(Steve, Couple 5)*

Others described a wider Church that was still not a safe and hospitable place to be, but one where there could be found pockets

163

of sanctuary. Their encounter with St Luke's had built their confidence and provided them with a positive image of their local church.

> It [St Luke's] feels like a safe place to go.   *(Ruth, Couple 2)*

> I think that it shows how much the Church is divided at the moment. The local church near my home basically shuns me, whereas we come to St Luke's and we are made welcome as a couple.   *(Chris, Couple 4)*

> My view of the Church in general is that there are now pockets . . . we now have an experience, a positive experience and there are pockets of the Church where we can now be accepted as a same-sex couple. So it is at least possible to find a niche in the Church.   *(Amelia, Couple 2)*

Some, though looking for authorisation and blessing on their union, had found signs of faith stirring in them or recovery of faith that had been dormant for a period of time.

> We have both decided that we would like to come to church on occasions in the future. For me the experience has awakened some sort of spirituality in a sense. I hope that it is something that will develop actually.   *(Ian, Couple 5)*

> I have been away from the Church for quite a while now, but I feel firmer in my beliefs now than at any time. A return to the Church through this ceremony has got me thinking again and drawn me closer to God.   *(Stephen, Couple 6)*

Some voices saw the open policy of local churches like St Luke's as a challenge to a wider Church that would either not address the issue of who they were, or preferred to keep gay and lesbian partnership so silent as to be effectively ignored.

> Obviously we feel a lot for St Luke's. I wouldn't say that my views of the institutional church have changed particularly.

If we went to a lot of other places we would still be turned away. But I felt relaxed and accepted at St Luke's and that was the main thing.   *(Paul, Couple 4)*

I am very pleased that St Luke's will do ceremonies for same-sex couples because it is nice to know that the doors really are open to anyone. Others in the wider Church need to know that life goes on and that they need to accept people for who they are in life. God said that you should love one another.   *(Douglas, Couple 6)*

Douglas and Paul each highlight a problem that has dogged the Church at every level in the debate on same-gender partnerships. They both know that there is no single view on where gay and lesbian couples stand within the Church and that some parts of the Church appear quite hostile on this issue. Churches seeking to engage in the pastoral care of any minority group will have to face questions dealing with conflict and power and their perceptions of authority. What happens when opposite points of view come into conflict with each other? What should the local church do when it finds itself at odds with what some other parts of the wider Church seem to think, perhaps even the hierarchical leadership of the Church? If 'doing the Christian thing' reveals a model of God as a compassionate, non-violent resister of injustice, it needs somehow to be held within the framework of that wider Church.

What I am going to suggest now is that any church community seeking to exercise a ministry of pastoral care and support will encounter three different aspects of that pastoral care. The first will be to see pastoral care as protest. The blessing of same-gender partners, while seeking to care for the couple in the local context, does not enjoy universal support in other contexts. It will lead to conflict. How that conflict is handled will be a mark of how well the local church can live up to its image of non-violent resistance. The second will be to see pastoral care as an encounter of trans-formation. The open support of lesbian and gay couples will have an undoubted effect upon them. Their voices have already witnessed to a changing perception of the Church, but what will the encounter have done for them as people? In what ways will their lives be changed through this practical engagement with the Church at a local level? The third will be to see pastoral care as a catalyst for genuine Church unity. How is it that we can be different and celebrate that difference without fragmenting? How can local church communities exercise ministries that are some-times perceived as contentious and yet remain cohesive communities, committed to the wider Church? What does such a model of unity have to offer other levels of the Church?

Pastoral care as protest

Amongst those writing critically on issues of authority and the Church, liberation theology scholars have highlighted the tensions very effectively. In what was quite radical work at the time, Leonardo Boff captured the mood for change in the Church that ultimately identified the stark imbalance of power in the authority structures of the Roman Catholic Church. The poor who occupied the baseline of the Church formed the overwhelming majority of the Church. Yet it was they who had least say in how it was run. The process of establishing and understanding base communities began to address issues of poverty and education. It raised social and political consciousness in a way that gave a voice to the poor majority. What was perceived initially as open rebellion towards an established authority structure became a movement in which the concerns of the poor featured prominently on the leadership agenda. What is at issue here is whether the same framework can be applied to the perceived 'poor' of the pastoral situation we have been reflecting on in this book. Can we highlight those same tensions in a local context and on the specific issue of blessing same-sex unions to help gay and lesbian partners who have no current legal status and security?

The methods involved in researching this book have been adopted from the base communities to enable a large sample of St Luke's congregation and a proportion of gay and lesbian couples to be heard publicly. It should be noted that it was *not* an intended feature of liberation theology to set out to address the power structures. The changes in those structures (such as they were) came about as a second order consequence of base communities attending to their direct needs. It is almost certain that the blessing of same-sex couples at a local level will reveal tensions, and might even bring the local church community into conflict with those in higher positions of recognised authority. Furthermore, I am clear that as is the case for the base communities, St Luke's is not, in the first instance, intending to attack the House of Bishops of the Church of England. Its primary purpose is in wanting to attend to the needs of its ministry to same-sex couples.

The church members revealed a high level of awareness of these tensions. As seen previously in the discussion on how the Church does the work of theology, the grass roots membership of the local church perceived authority as emanating from the top of the Church and making its way down to the base. Some of these views were positive; others were announced in hesitant tones. Roger made a clear declaration that being part of the Church of England was important and that there was danger for any single con-gregation setting itself apart from the wider Church in its thinking and teaching. Wally asked whether permission needs to be obtained from the diocesan authorities. Moira was uncertain about where a local church community would stand if it were perceived to be acting in direct defiance of its bishop.

Overall there was a clear mandate from the church members that their local church, based on its experiences over 20 years, had a responsibility to continue its support of gay and lesbian couples. It would do this by blessing their unions even if it was out of step with the voiced opinions of the leadership of the wider Church. Seventy-two per cent were in favour of a practice that had emerged from the experience that they had spent 20 years reflecting on. Four per cent of the church members were against the continuation. The remaining 24 per cent were undecided as to whether it was right to continue in such circumstances. Some of this indecision may arise from a sense of confusion as to where the centre of the

Church's authority is. For some, localised authority is a short cut to the kind of congregationalism that is not part of the Anglican identity. For others, there can be no directives given from the base of the Church to the top. This was a predominating view amongst the ethnic minority members. Eighty per cent of those interviewed in this category were undecided as to whether the local church could act against the common mind of its hierarchical leaders. Most agreed that gay and lesbian people could live as couples and be a blessing to those around them, and they all thought that gay and lesbian people could be blessed as individuals. However, on the issue of blessing them as couples they appealed to three different levels of authority.

As already noted, there was the appeal to the authority of Scripture: for Penny it was clear that the Scriptures forbade the coupling of men with men and women with women. It was contrary to creation and the purposes of God for human beings. Her experience was that some people of her cultural context and ethnicity avoided coming to St Luke's because the services of blessing existed.

Secondly there was the appeal to the authority of ecclesial consensus and civil law. Brenda noted that other churches 'don't like the idea'. She thought that it was a subject that did not promote the interests of Christian unity, and this was something that St Luke's as a local church should actively pursue. The promotion of this kind of unity was one that would bring about greater understanding through active dialogue. When the aim has been achieved in theory, there would be a harmonious context for pastoral action, but her view was that this required more debate and persuasion on the part of St Luke's: when everybody is doing it, St Luke's can do it too. Furthermore, it is not currently within the bounds of the law to protect such unions. When it becomes the law of the land she would be happy for it to happen in church. This raises a further question. How might the shaping of any social infrastructure that has a legal framework to protect it be influenced or changed? In this instance, how do gay couples who are unprotected in law and do not enjoy the same rights as their married, heterosexual counterparts, come to enjoy those rights and securities? The suggestion here seems to be that the Church is led by the initiatives of the State, but I am not convinced that this is the way law is created or reformed.

Finally there was the appeal to the authority of the clerical hierarchy. Sandra's was a frustrating point of view in that she seemed to perceive an injustice in this matter, but the leaders had spoken and so what could anyone do?

> Us as members, what can we put to the leaders of the Church or the head of the Church?   (*Sandra, C4*)

The resignation of this statement is compelling. It suggests a gulf between the thinking and experience of a grass roots church and a national leadership that is perceived as not in touch with it. The voices of ethnic minority groups have long gone unheard both in the Church and in Western culture at large. That 80 per cent of those interviewed in this category were unable to come to a decision is perhaps a reflection of the frustration felt by some of the most silenced people on the baseline of the Church. Others who have suffered similarly have managed to find a voice and effect some form of change in the social order to allow their lives to be freer and more fulfilled. The Women's Movement and the rise of feminist consciousness occupied a prominent role in Western European and North American culture. Perhaps its greatest gift to all levels of society was its capacity to educate. Tina's was the only voice amongst those interviewed from the ethnic minority category that spoke in support of this praxis and was upbeat in holding her view. For her the key to change was precisely this capacity to educate. To support gay and lesbian couples openly and in a practical manner was principally an educative act. Individual liberty could only be brought about by a raising to consciousness of the injustices experienced by gay and lesbian couples. What is emerging here is a picture of a local church community that wants to remain within the wider Church and finds enormous value in it. However, it is a church community that has noted an unjust situation for gay and lesbian people within it and within society at large. It is also a community that has had a positive experience of gay and lesbian couples within the congregation and in a wider ministry. This is notably revealed in the experience of the greater majority of the church members. It is they who seem to have an inclination to peaceful resistance and open support of gay and lesbian couples.

In 1990 Walter Righter, acting as an assistant bishop in the Episcopal Diocese of Newark, USA, knowingly ordained a gay man who lived with his partner in a committed relationship. It was not the first ordination of its kind nor the most publicised but in 1995 a small group of fellow bishops brought heresy charges against Righter for what he had done. The trial lasted 16 months and concluded that no 'core doctrine' had been violated. In that time Righter reflected on what he perceived to be major connections between misogyny and homophobia, and how the Church's treatment of women had impacted upon its attitude towards and pastoral care of gay men and lesbian women.[10]

This rings important bells for the local church community under scrutiny here. St Luke's has a long history of supporting the ministry of women and particularly of those wishing to be ordained to the priesthood. This only became a final reality for Anglicans in England in 1994. However, St Luke's had on its parish staff a woman who was admitted to the (lay) order of deaconess (so not *ordained* a deacon) in 1978 – the same year as Rodney and Saxon arrived in the parish. Liz Canham had long wished to see her vocation to the priesthood tested and realised. Her story is very much a part of the local church story too. Liz eventually went to the United States to train and to be ordained as a priest in 1981. Lavinia picks up the threads of connection and uses them as a major argument to continue pastoral practices that might bring about confrontation with figures of authority.

> The reason I say yes positively is that St Luke's supported and actively encouraged the ministry of women when the ordination of women was a dream and when the [wider] Church did not support women in the priesthood. St Luke's

> still went ahead with Liz Canham and having women cele-
> brate as and when it was possible and were out of step with
> the main church . . . We have a Gospel about love and
> justice and these people are committed to each other [same-
> sex couples] and want to have that confirmed in church at
> a blessing. I think that we should have the courage to carry
> on doing it.   *(Lavinia, C1)*

To the cynical this may seem as no more than posturing: a local
church decides to thumb its nose at the wider Church. However,
a glance at the church archives for that period reveals that St
Luke's was simply acting consistently with its overall approach to
pastoral care.

The church received a good deal of publicity from local newspapers on one other major issue during this period at the end of
the 1970s. The celebration of gay unions and the ordination
of women to the priesthood were preceded by a commitment to
support divorcees who wished to marry for a second time in
church while their first marital partner was still alive. Re-marriage
of divorcees and the ordination of women to the priesthood were
critical issues that were debated by the General Synod of the
Church of England. In both instances the synod allowed for an
appeal to conscience to take place at a local level. Clergy and local
churches that did not wish to allow the marriage of those who had
been divorced were not obliged to officiate at such ceremonies. To
this day there are still multifarious practices in each of the parishes
of the Church of England. So too we find something similar with
the ordination of women to the priesthood. Elaborate plans were
made to secure the consciences of those who were opposed to
General Synod's vote to proceed with legislation to allow women
to be ordained. Anglicans were told that they had to live with 'two
integrities' and each parish could pass its own resolution. Either it
would receive the ministry of a woman priest or it could choose
not to.

To sum up, in the late 1970s St Luke's, Charlton took a consistent
line on three important pastoral issues that lay before the wider

Church. It seems to me that in so doing this, this local church was merely maintaining an ethos in practice and purpose that has shaped its entire pastoral ministry. The issues emerged in the first instance from practical and personal encounters. Twenty years later, the remarriage of a divorcee is still a matter of personal conscience for the individual priest and his/her church council. As with the ordination of women to the priesthood there is an absence of consensus in the wider Church. It is perhaps unrealistic to expect that there should be. What has happened though is that a national Church has recognised that there are some issues that cannot be legislated for from the 'top down'. Here are two instances that affect the life of the whole Church that can only begin to resolve themselves in the light of local context and experience. The question remains; if it can be so for remarriage and ordination, both of which have all kinds of doctrinal apparatus attached to them, why can the issue of blessing same-sex partnerships (not nearly so encumbered) not be devolved in the same way? Members of the church were quite quick to see that this was a sensible way to proceed.

> It is nice that an individual has a bit of autonomy to accept the needs of their community. It is not suitable to have same-sex blessings in every church, but if the congregation accepts that . . .   *(Sara, C3)*

> . . . there are many issues and things in church life where things within the same denomination differ. This may be one of them. It isn't just a human moral decision; it is a question of where you have got to in your church family life with God at the core. It includes prayer and looking to see what you think God's purpose for that particular church is. It might be different. I don't think it should deflect us from what we feel.   *(Mary, C2)*

The development of local theologies acknowledges the variation of context and the way they impact upon the community under scrutiny. I would consider that in approaching the question of blessing same-sex relationships it is probably a more honest way for the Church to proceed if it is to offer any kind of care and support for lesbian and gay couples that is both practical and generous. This contrasts quite vividly with the attempts of the bishops themselves in the publication of their discussion document *Issues In Human Sexuality*. It is a document that works hard to find consensus where there is none. That one of its objectives seems to have been to provide a picture of broad agreement amongst the bishops themselves is a principal weakness. Operating a principle of two integrities at least exposes the virtue of honest disagreement and a commitment to living with those differences while we try to understand why those differences are important. I do not consider it to be a permanent solution, but it is a way to create lengthy periods of reflection. This is a lesson that the wider Church already knows and has experience of in the examples indicated.

In 'doing the Christian thing', the St Luke's church community experiences the tension of discerning what it considers to be the right pastoral action for a particular situation, with how it manages to hold together as a cohesive community of people. It's pastoral action is well received by the lesbian and gay couples who come to make vows of commitment and who say that they feel strengthened in that commitment through God's blessing. The congregational voices and those of the couples sing in harmony at this point.

The church members felt moved to continue this support, despite knowing that other parts of the wider Church were hostile in their condemnation of it. Senior members, intermediate members and the newest members were all 80 per cent in support of the current practice continuing. The young people of the church were 100 per cent in support of the practice continuing whereas the ethnic minority members were 60 per cent opposed. Taken as an overall total, 72 per cent of those interviewed were in support of the practice continuing, 16 per cent were against and 12 per cent were undecided.

Church members were keen to support the ministry to same-gender couples but were also keen to see that this ministry undertook good practices that could be reflected across the spectrum of its pastoral ministry. However, they were also concerned that St Luke's might be perceived by some as a 'single issue church'. From the contextual evidence gathered I think this would be a difficult charge to sustain. As I have already outlined the issue of same-sex partnerships was but one of three major 'sexuality and relational' issues tackled by the local church community in the last 20 years. In all three a consistent approach saw strong emphasis on the value of the pastoral encounter.

The members felt that an ethos for 'good practice' should be one that strikes a balance between what is charged by some to be 'openness' and by others as 'brazenness'. The problems attending the level of publicity that occurred in 1979 when Saxon and Rodney held their service of covenanted union and blessing are well reflected in a personal memo of the then Bishop of Southwark, Mervyn Stockwood to the Rector of St Luke's at that time, Tony Crowe.

> As you know, I have a liberal attitude towards these matters . . . but I try to take into consideration those who hold contrary views. That is why I think one has to treat the subject with great delicacy and not to be insensitive. I regret much of what is done by the Gay Liberation Movement, especially in the Church. If two men believe that they are justified in living together and if they wish to ask God's blessing on their commitment, I think it best for a priest to say prayers with them privately. The time may come when the Church will take a different attitude, but at the moment a public ceremony can do nothing but make a difficult situation more difficult.[11]

Certainly in 1979 the level of press and public interest in what was happening at St Luke's and its support for gay and lesbian couples led to the 'open' styled service (as experienced by Rodney and Saxon) relocating and becoming more quietly 'private'. It was a situation that continued for 14 years.

By 1999 a mood of change had come about for many in the

church. There was a greater sympathy for more openness while recognising the need to exercise some prudence. By contrast with Roger and Millie who see this work as a clergy initiative backed by the authority of the lay-elected PCC, June and Mary reflect on extending the role of the laity in administering such services. This would be consistent with the greater role of the laity generally in preparing *all* kinds of pastoral offices and worship services.

> I think that we should be treating them just the same as anyone else who comes to church for a blessing. If you appoint someone special to deal with this, then you are making this a special case aren't you? I agree that it should be open and have more lay people involved. *(June, C2)*

> I don't see why the laity shouldn't be more involved. Some of us were invited to the blessing of two Italian ladies. That was very important because I think that the whole point of a blessing in church is that it is not a private thing with the priest and the couple . . . *(Mary, C2)*

Openness was distinguished from the promotional activity of strident advertising. What people seemed to value most was that the local church community represented the local community. Sara describes it as being a local church with a local ministry.

> I would hate to see St Luke's being simply named as the place where gay couples go. It's like people from all over London coming to be blessed. I think if the people are local or fairly local . . . then it might be appropriate. *(Sara, C3)*

This is an important point for all churches with a commitment to local pastoral practice.

Pastoral care as transformation

Gay and lesbian couples who approach St Luke's for services of blessing are invited into a process of preparation. During the four sessions they are asked to talk about each other, and why they have made an approach to the established Church for their blessing ceremony. As has already been seen, most are looking for a place of safety where they can make simple vows of commitment in public. They wish to be identified with each other as a couple and for their change of status to be recognised by friends and family and taken seriously. However, it would be true to say that there are a variety of venues that they could choose. Why then come to the Church? Many of the couples have already described their anxiety in approaching the Church for a service of covenanted union and blessing. Indeed for those who do make the approach, there are many more that do not, preferring instead to mark their lifestyles in quite different ways. Some of the couples had experience of homophobic discrimination within the Church. Amelia and Ruth had attended a baptism where they had been invited to stand as godparents. This had not pleased the priest who made his displeasure evident. So, why did they bother?

None of the couples taking part in this reflection stated from the outset that they had come to the Church for a service of blessing because they were looking for God. What became clear as the sessions proceeded was that like many people that do not live within the centre of the church community, they were unfamiliar with most elements of religious language. This is not at all uncommon. There are countless people outside formal church communities (and some within) for whom words like redemption, salvation, eschatology, atonement and grace mean nothing at all. As already seen, the language of 'blessing' was far easier to substitute with the language of 'marriage', whether it was marriage that was sought or not. This does not denote a liberality on my part or a misconception on theirs, it merely describes what the Church has done with the language of faith. For most people it is inaccessible. It remains a piece of ecclesial baggage that is locked up in the Church and is not part of everyday language.

What the voices of the couples all spoke for, was the experience of feeling different about life following their encounter with the church community and their service of blessing. As they reflected upon the process that they had gone through what emerged in their thinking were quiet testimonies of how faith mattered to them and how they struggled to understand what it means to believe in God. Naming the matters of faith emerged in everyday language. It was neither self-conscious piety nor embarrassing 'religious-speak', but instead a quite touching account of what they felt deeply about but were usually disinclined to raise in everyday conversation.

For many of the couples, this encounter with the Church allowed them to revisit and think again about the images of God that they had either grown up with or adopted in the course of life.

> For me God, or the Light, having been with me never left me. So wherever I have been the light was there and with all those people. They are good people [she is referring to the members of St Luke's who came to support her blessing ceremony with Daniela]. They pray the same God. God is here, is with me. I see God in a plant or an animal, in the rain or the clouds, any beautiful thing I see God. I don't think that the Church is going to change my thinking about God. *(Christina, Couple 1)*

Christina's description of God might have been plucked from a handbook of Celtic Christian imagery, yet as an Italian it is unlikely to have been formed thus. On the contrary, she seems to suggest that her ability to find God in the signs of creation is likely to be contrary to the images of God defined by the teaching of the Church. The Church as an institution is something that she has left behind her, finding it clerically dominated, hierarchically formed and redundant in what it has to tell her of God. Instead the images of creation and the creatures of God are the signs of God, whom she describes as the Light.

Steve, who has strongly appreciated the 'human face' of the Church he has found in his encounter, makes a similar pitch. Unlike Christina's location of God in the language of creation, Steve's experience brings him to the conclusion that God is to be found in the midst of community. Though he would never describe it as such, he offers a very incarnational image of God.

177

> Coming to St Luke's for the blessing service has made me
> think about life and other people and how important other
> people are. There are lots of different people in life and it
> is important not to make assumptions. One thing that
> impressed me was we came and had a look around St
> Luke's and all the people were there. They were just ordinary
> everyday people who are perfectly happy to take other
> people at face value. There was a great feeling of together-
> ness and I think that God is togetherness amongst people.
> I probably didn't realise that before. My spirituality and vision
> of God is found in other people.   *(Steve, Couple 5)*

Steve is surprised by his own discovery. He finds God in relationships and describes this as 'togetherness' in the community. For
him this is brought to birth by the experience of being accepted
by that community. By it, his view of Church is transformed. He
finds a language for God that neither diminishes his feelings about
the encounter, nor trivialises his new discovery.

The positive nature of their encounter with the local church
transformed the thinking of others too. Chris had already described
a Christian upbringing and one that he had sought to rediscover
as an adult in his nearest local church. Some members of that
church community had particularly upset him upon his admission
to them that he was gay. He was no longer allowed to help with
the junior church and was made to feel that unless he altered his
behavioural instincts and adopted a celibate lifestyle, he risked
eternal damnation. Unlike Paul, his partner, Chris had needed a
degree of self-persuasion before risking an approach to the Church
for a service of blessing. Contrasting the experiences of the two
local churches Chris was able to see that entire church communities
are able to influence perceptions of God.

> Going back to my experience of the response I had from
> the church around the corner, I remember that I went on the
> course that they offered because I wanted to know more. I
> had certain beliefs and it mixed me up as to what God was.
> I was thinking, well how could I be gay? It was not a

choice I had made. I am gay and if God has made me and is allowing me to have these feelings, then why am I also being told by the Church that I am not allowed to love someone? That mixed me up to be honest. I was very confused. It was like the image of God I got from that church was very dictatorial. I had to conform because God was very selective in whom he accepted. Coming to St Luke's, I have found an image of God that was welcoming of anybody. *(Chris, Couple 4)*

Chris's recovery is brought about by a positive experience of hospitality in the shape of a church community that does not treat him as a sexual predator or potential child abuser, but instead welcomes him. God the dictator, who had been conveyed to him by one church community as repressive (take a celibate lifestyle) and unloving (you are made with these feelings but you can't express them in a wholesome loving way), is transformed. Instead, Chris experiences the security of acceptance and is enabled to replace a despotic image of God with one that accepts and welcomes him. His partner Paul summarises it in his straightforward assessment that 'God is love'.

For Ian, 'doing the Christian thing' meant actively looking for these positive models of God in the pastoral activity of the Church. Like Chris, he had previous experience of a repressive church community. He described these repressive features as ones held by a number of sects. What he valued in his experience with the Church was that it had the capacity to resist cultivating this kind of ethos.

When I was 16 I was roped in to join the Mormons and it was a very strange experience. I was very young and naïve and I got involved through a school-friend. It was at a time when my sexuality was just forming and they were just so repressive towards it. They would have been outraged by what we have done here at this church. Something like this is where the Church of England is really progressive. All the fringe religions and sects are anti-gay and quite horrific in their approach. They don't seem to me to be Christian at all. They are not looking at people as people or trying to understand why people act in a certain way. I think that part of what Christianity should be about is this thing about trying to understand people. *(Ian, Couple 5)*

What has been transforming for Ian is that his new encounter with the Church has altered the way he looks at life. His experience of preparing for a service of covenanted union with Steve was one that propelled him into re-evaluating the things that he had seen as important. Through this experience he seems to have discovered a Church that has listened to him and enabled him to address the questions of meaning and purpose that he wants his life to focus on.

As I get older I think about Christianity and it has become more important. Life is changing so much and there is so much pressure and things are not always changing for the better. Then I think you really do have to ask yourself what you are actually doing here and what is our purpose in life. I think that some sort of spirituality in life is important and without that you are really direction-less. It awoke something in me, preparing for this ceremony . . . and I think that what I have found has been strengthened by this. It is very hard to put into words. *(Ian, Couple 5)*

Acceptance and affirmation were features of ministry that all couples met in their encounter with the local church. For Anna and Karen reading this as a sign of God's affirmation and acceptance brought with it a heightened sense of responsibility. The service of blessing had become a place of reconciliation and new beginnings for them. Anna's tense relationship with her born-again Christian mother changed in the preparation period. The new relationship that she was to form with her partner's child was also a sign of the change that she had agreed to and now had to take responsibility for.

It has made me look on life differently. My family has

changed. I have responsibility for a child and my relationship with my own mother has changed. For God to look on that and say, yes, I am giving you those responsibilities and for me to accept them, I think that they may well be linked. I feel accepted and affirmed by God in that. *(Anna, Couple 3)*

For Karen, though she too felt changed by the encounter, it has been hard to shake off the powerful image of God she had in her childhood.

It has made me look on life a bit different. I have always believed in God, but God somehow remains very powerful and in charge of things like when I was brought up as a child. I suppose it was my Catholic upbringing! *(Karen, Couple 3)*

Acceptance provides a way into community life. For Amelia and Ruth this became more important after the birth of their first child, but the platform for it was secured in the preparation for their blessing ceremony. As with other couples, God was identified in terms of how they found the Church. Having found a way into an accepting church community, God was made available to them in a way that they had not felt before.

Certainly the way I think about life now is more wholesome. There are three of us now because we have just had a baby. So it has opened up my perspective on things. There is Amelia and me and the baby. So the Church and life and God is all open there for all of us now. I feel that because we were accepted then she will be too. *(Ruth, Couple 2)*

Lives met at the cutting edge of pastoral ministry will often be transformed. That is the nature of encounter. In the pastoral encounter, engagement takes place and lives are influenced and often changed. In the examples of pastoral care as transformation, positive images of God are planted in the lives of ordinary people enabling them to speak meaningfully on matters of faith and life. No new members were made for the congregation, but that was

181

not the purpose of the exercise. In serving a wider community the Church can be seen to make a difference.

Pastoral care as a catalyst for unity

While it may be important to note that there are occasions when pastoral care might lead to conflict and that lives might well be transformed as a result of it, the local church community was also well aware of the danger of division. It is unlikely that the Church at any level is going to be a body of total agreement but how is it possible to live in community and be able to disagree? Pastoral care is hardly that if it leads ultimately to needless schism. Those members of the church community who took part in this reflection exercise revealed a majority that were, broadly speaking, in favour of supporting those same-gender couples who seek blessing for their unions in St Luke's church. However, there were some who expressed uncertainties at the present time and a small number who were not in favour.

The capacity to live harmoniously even at points of disagreement was a concern for every one of the church members who shared their thoughts on the matter. Those who were most conservative in their views of blessing gay and lesbian couples in church were amongst those who were most anxious to find a common mind on the subject. Ultimately, although there was some confusion as to the actual place of gay and lesbian couples in the open structures of church life, there was no question of asking active gay and lesbian couples to find another church. Those in the ethnic minority category all used the language of education, prayer and discussion as a means of furthering common understanding and representing differing views.

Only Roger and Arthur outside the ethnic minority category expressed a degree of misgiving as to how St Luke's represented its stance on this issue and its relationship to the wider Church. Both adopted a 'traditional' model of Church and hierarchy. Arthur was resigned to being in a minority on the subject in his local church community and thought that the only way that things might change was through the establishment of a new 'doctrine' that might affect the policy and practices of local churches. Roger held a slightly different view of the Church. However, he was keen to see that the local church did not remain out of step with the wider Church. His views contrasted with those others offered at this point not because of their conclusions but because of their *approach* to the matter.

Here we have two different approaches creating a tension. The first starts from theory. Its language tends to be technical rather than personal and it is often academic in style. People thinking in this way tend to describe sexual intimacy as 'homosexual acts'. The second starts from experience. This approach, in contrast, will often rely upon personal stories. The language is sometimes emotive and more conversational in style, and sexual activity will be described in relational language. This distinction was seen to be important as discussion was agreed by all to be a generally welcome thing but there often seemed to be no way of bridging the difference between these two approaches. For the church members it was clear that a starting point was necessary, but which one should they take? Could any such discussion on blessing same-gender partnerships take place without taking note of this? Whatever the starting point, they recognised that it would have some considerable effect on the way in which people engaged in the educational process of discussion. For members of St Luke's church community it was also formative in their understanding of what it means to be Church. In other words, how they engaged in the discussion on gay and lesbian couples and managed to disagree without falling out with each other was all part of 'doing the Christian thing'.

Some saw this as critical to parish community life. The community discovered that discussion worked best without hysteria. Surely it was possible to be passionate without being hysterical? The church members recognised the value of this in what they saw around them. Perhaps the fact that it had been a personal issue (rather than an abstract and theoretical one) for more than 20 years made some difference.

> I suppose that St Luke's has influenced me in that when I
> hear other people talking about the subject they seem more
> uptight about it. I have never felt particularly anti, but I do
> know people who are without knowing much about it.
> *(Doreen, C1)*

As a congregation of people who have remained together despite
disagreement, St Luke's might be persuaded that the reason why
there is no major fall-out over this particular issue is because it
has always been just one issue of church life amongst many others.
It has been a part of church consciousness for so long it is practi-
cally not an issue at all. There is greater loyalty to remaining in
the local church perceived as a whole, than in dividing over partial
and particular issues.

> So people who are really anti say well it has sort of happened
> in the past, we don't like it but we don't want to leave the
> church we have attended for so long. Their loyalty to their
> church is perhaps more important than one particular
> issue. *(James, C1)*

> In life, irrespective of whether you are in church or anywhere
> else, you are going to find a conflict of interest and quite
> often it is just a question of getting used to them. *(Arthur,
> C2)*

> There are always going to be differing views on various
> issues and that is fine. *(Sara, C3)*

Those who have engaged in the debate on homosexual relations
in the Church of England have not always dealt so generously
with those of differing views. Some of that may be because in
entering such a discussion, the size of the debate and the various
levels of entry mean that simple basics like the clarification of
terms of reference complicate the discussion from the outset. The
General Synod debate of 1987 saw no real meeting of minds and
the debate became acrimonious and hurtful. In 1998, the bishops

of the Lambeth Conference fared no better. It was hardly surprising given the cultural diversity that was represented at the conference. There were some who considered 'political baggage' to have held sway too.

> There are persistent rumours that the anti-homosexual alliance has been mobilised and is being co-ordinated by American right wing evangelicals. In return for funding meetings of bishops from the developing world . . . It is claimed that American evangelical bishops promised to support a tough stand on international debt in return for the developing world bishops taking up the crusade against homosexuality.[12]

This debate was also acrimonious and on its conclusion the press and general public were treated to an extraordinary spectacle as Bishop Emmanuel Chukwumu, of Enugu in Nigeria, attempted a deliverance ministry on the secretary of the Lesbian and Gay Christian Movement at the entrance to the debating hall.

There are fundamental differences between the General Synod of the Church of England and the Lambeth Conference of the bishops of the Anglican Communion, and the local church community of St Luke's, Charlton. The first is that neither the elected members of synod nor those called to the conference could describe the bodies they represent as 'communities'. The local church in Charlton can do this. It is not a body of like-minded people but it is one in which the members have made a commitment to living alongside each other in their diversity and difference. Thus it is in a powerful position to make decisions and policies by reflecting upon common experiences. The common experience of 20 years ago was that Saxon and Rodney arrived in the parish and joined the church community. There was no cause to debate homosexual acts in an abstract and theoretical way. Twenty years later that foundation has led to a community of people reflecting together to see how this story has been inculcated within the whole church story. Ironically by reflecting upon a common experience, there has been less opportunity for schism within the membership of the local church itself. It begins with a common reality; the terms of reference are agreed, everyone knows who Saxon and Rodney were and most know who the current gay and lesbian members are. The second factor that helps the membership hold together while experiencing conflicting views is the ability to own up to knowing someone who is gay. Church members have drawn on the experience of not only having friends that are lesbian or gay, but also having family members that are. What this process of reflection has done is to open up a window of opportunity for this community now to share its experience. That is the purpose of this book. What we have here is an example of pastoral care and pastoral reflection in action. The openness of the perceived pastoral care and the ability to reflect upon it with a similar degree of openness, are crucial ingredients in the pursuit of unity. In doing this, the church community continues its quest for what it understands of itself and its task of what it means to be 'doing the Christian thing'.

CHAPTER 7

Voices Speaking Truth to Power

a community of inclusion –
towards a new vision of healing

In the reflection process so far we have listened to the voices of a church community retrieving an important part of its own story and reflecting upon its 20-year history of supporting lesbian and gay partnerships. The church members have not only been able to thus reflect on a ministry to same-gender couples, but they have also revealed their commitment to continue to live as a community marked by difference and diversity. Those lesbian and gay couples that have also taken part in this reflection experience of meeting the church in a ministry of blessing have endorsed the value of this ministry. Many have described wounded feelings of alienation and marginalisation that have been met and tended in their encounter with St Luke's, perhaps suggesting that this has been possible because of an implicit understanding that to be a community of wholeness and healing is primarily to be inclusive. The images with which the church members describe themselves, the church story and the ministry it espouses are indicating factors in this conclusion. Significantly they are images that are similar to those used by the couples to describe their perceptions of God through the agency of the Church. We are left to consider that a ministry containing the principal characteristics of welcome, safety and liberation in the images of hospitality, sanctuary and empowerment is of considerable importance if it claims to be one that leads people into a place of wholeness and healing.

Part 1 Retrieving a political healing ministry

Images, symbols and idols

Just how the church community is able to undertake the task of reflecting upon a pastoral practice to support same-gender couples and be able to continue as an integrated community emerges in the picture images it has used to describe its ethos and ministry. As already noted, themes of hospitality, sanctuary and empowerment consistently arose in the description that each of the church partici- pants made. All of these themes were reinforced by the views of the couples and furthered in their own perceptions of an important church story that was in need of recovery. The story of Rodney Madden and Saxon Lucas was not merely one of St Luke's first openly gay couple wanting a blessing service to mark their relationship. It was one that described the people involved in the images of the local church ethos they had found and joined. The recovery of the Rodney and Saxon story 20 years after it was first lived and told is one that compels us to take symbolism seriously when identifying story images. The re-telling of their story has allowed those images of hospitality, sanctuary and empowerment to emerge.

Towards a re-reading of the Church's healing ministry

> Hermeneutics seems to me to be animated by this double motivation: willingness to suspect, willingness to listen: vow of rigor, vow of obedience. In our time we have not finished doing away with *idols* and we have barely begun to listen to *symbols*.[1]

At the start of his major work, *Binding the Strong Man*, Ched Myers adopts this quote from Paul Ricoeur to illustrate his point that biblical criticism has lost its way in interpreting the gospels for ordinary Christian worshippers who meet in our churches week by week. It is a significant quote in the context of this enterprise in that it can equally be applied to the way we do the work of interpreting our lives as communities of Christian action with particular reference to healing and wholeness. Within this ministry there has, in my view, been a serious loss of insight into the power of symbol and imagery and a deferment to an inherited view of healing and wholeness that has become idolatrous. This inheritance has emerged in part because churches in Europe and North America have bought into a culture that is very individualistic and 'client centred'. This view is one that might be seen reflected in much contemporary pastoral theology in general and literature on the healing ministry in particular. Much pastoral theology became the preserve of the pastoral counselling movement that grew through the 1960s and 1970s.

> As the British writer R. A. Lambourne noted in his paper 'With love to the U.S.A.' at the beginning of the 1970s, counselling and humanistic psychology appear to have ousted all other ways of understanding or helping human beings.[2]

For a Church suffering a loss of identity, decreasing numbers and a drop in vocations to the ordained ministry this was very attractive. It could find purpose and meaning for pastoral ministry and ministers in a culture that was becoming increasingly individualistic. It is no real surprise that the ministry of healing, which had revived to a degree at the turn of the century, began a renaissance at about this time.

Today, if you visit almost any theological bookstore, it is most likely that you will find a substantial section given over to the healing ministry. What you will also find is that the bulk of the literature on sale will reflect a similar ethos. It will preoccupy the reader with accounts of individual healing and success stories. In North America this ethos has translated well for the Charismatic movement within the powerful medium of television and the advent of the TV evangelist. However, I would want to advance the view that all churches with a serious commitment to the ministry of healing run the risk of idolising this ministry if we do not recover a broader sense of what it means to *live as a healing community*. What I want to suggest in this chapter is that, with a fresh look at Scripture, St Luke's church, in its support for gay and lesbian couples, is a radical model of a Christian healing community because of its commitment to being an inclusive community. I want further to suggest that it is precisely because it can be described as a community of healing that it manages to stay together as a community. For this I will require a new tool of interpretation.

Healing: the body and the body politic – a political hermeneutic

Healing is often perceived as a 'religious' activity in Christian circles. It is something that is generally seen to be a good thing. It is not seen as something that brings its ministers into conflict with the secular authorities. It is not regarded as a political vehicle. Western European and North American cultures have, by and large, managed to maintain a distinct separation of the political and religious world which the cultures of Eastern Europe and the Southern hemisphere are baffled by. Ched Myers, in his review of the healing narratives in the Gospel of Mark, asks the question: why then does the healing ministry of Jesus lead to his execution? He finds an answer by detecting a triangular relationship in each of the healing stories in Mark's gospel narrative. The most obvious is the relationship between Jesus and whoever it is that comes for healing. We might describe this as a client-system relationship. However, there are other systems at play that are revealed in a second relationship: that of the excluded and what she or he identifies as an oppressive (or excluding) system.

Healing: the activity of inclusion

I wish to be clear that those who come for healing are not simply sick in the sense of having poor or broken health, nor is it merely

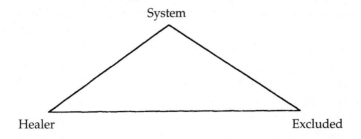

System

Healer   Excluded

a cure that they seek. A new understanding of healing is required when reading these gospel stories and drawing parallels in this research. Those like the leper (Mark 1:40–45 – my primary illustration) or Legion or the unnamed woman healed of a blood flow are a category of excluded who stand outside accepted and acceptable human society. In each case the excluded approach Jesus not to ritually defile him or because they have nothing to lose but because they see something in him. Jesus is proximate and is consistently so to all those who were placed outside of society. This raises all sorts of questions about Christian discipleship and what it means to be approachable in life. If the sole understanding of healing is seen as *cure*, as of sickness, then we adopt a singular (and in my opinion narrow) view of healing. An altered view of healing instead focuses upon the effect of *exclusion*. It is the implication of re-including the excluded within community life that is a hidden healing dynamic. If these stories can be read through the political lens suggested, they reveal issues (other than blood, skin-disfigurement and psychological breakdown/possession) that cause discrimination and exclusion. These are revealed as issues of race and gender, which present themselves in the tense relationship between the human body and the body politic.

Most societies and cultures can provide examples of people who are included or excluded on the basis of ethnicity, gender or sexual orientation. For Jesus the healer, whatever stance he takes towards the excluded in each story, he is put in relation to the body politic because of that stance. In Mark 1:40ff the leper asks principally to be declared clean (rather than cured). This is in keeping with the

Levitical codes where leprosy is 'resolved' by going to the priest and undergoing an elaborate process of ritual purification.[3] This was not by any means a 'cure' but was instead a means of re-admission into and recognition by society as a member of it.

How can these insights be properly applied in the case of same-sex couples seeking the blessing of the church for their union? The immediate danger is one of misunderstanding. A misapplication of the text might suggest to some that this reflection now concludes that gay and lesbian people are as lepers, the mad or ritually unclean (which it does not). That danger is increased if healing is perceived as no more than the *cure* of individuals. This work nowhere implies that gay and lesbian couples need to be cured of a pathological condition. Healing, read with the political her-meneutic I have borrowed from Myers, becomes a community activity in which the excluded are included within the family of that community. Then the healing action becomes the prerogative of the whole community with benefits for both the community and any excluded from it. The Marcan healing stories emphasise this. Unless those excluded from the community are restored to it, the community itself is not whole. Gay and lesbian people might need healing, but no more than anyone else. In the gospel encounter with Jesus the healer, the excluded are declared included and encouraged to live openly as full members of the society/ community in which they wish to live.

The main problem that we have here is that Jesus is not licensed to make such pronouncements. He has not had the authority passed down to him to declare who is included and who is not included within Jewish society. But he has an authority – and this is recognised by the excluded, the leper, who himself has chosen to bypass the 'established' authority of the priestly caste. The leper recognises that Jesus stands in a different relationship to him (his body) and the body politic. The pastoral action that Jesus then takes is to *touch* the very body that has been rejected. In doing so he challenges the whole Jewish system that has determined which relationships are acceptable and what the terms and conditions of those relationships are to be. Jesus then sends the leper off to the priests. We usually read this as a means by which Jesus has his action 'legitimised' by the existing power structures, but this really makes no sense. What the text actually says is that the leper is to go and witness *(martyrion)* to the priests. One translation of the term 'witness' is 'speaking truth to power'. The leper can do this because he has recognised in Jesus his willingness to 'accept' him and has found the place of 'sanctuary' in making the encounter. By returning to the priests he can confront the system because he has been 'empowered'. The leper is now the subject of his own liberation rather than a passive recipient of healing as a client. All should end well here, except that what actually happens is that he goes away and tells the world instead. It is others who inform the established authorities. One not 'authorised' in the recognised way has made the declaration of inclusion. The healer becomes a threat to the establishment authorities.

The point of this extensive piece of scriptural analysis at this stage is to ask some basic questions. If there is good reason for reading the healing 'miracles' of Jesus with such a political hermeneutic, can it be argued that the ongoing practice of blessing same-gender partners at St Luke's is a sign of inclusiveness and of the ministry of healing argued for here? To answer this I will now address some images of perceived healing suggested by the church members and couples participating in the reflection.

Healing as hospitality

The first image is located in the gospel story we have just looked at: the observation that the initiative and request for transformation lay with the person seeking ministry. This was possible because the client recognised the characteristic of approachability in the perceived healer. The first image of self-description used by the church members from St Luke's was an image of hospitality. They spoke of what they perceived as a warm welcoming church. So did the couples. They described warmth, friendliness and acceptance. For many of the members these were things that had been their experience too upon arrival. Some of them had arrived at critical moments in their lives. Jennifer had come following a bereavement, Lavinia had come following a personal crisis, Doreen and Moira had each been living and working in another country and were trying to find 'home' again, Sally had suffered a petrol bomb attack on her home by the racist BNP. Amongst the couples some recounted previous experiences of rejection. Chris had been told to suppress his gay feelings and felt shunned by his nearest church. Ruth had been 'rejected' as a godparent by the priest at a baptism. So some have the experience of isolation, if not exclusion by certain sections of society. The initial subject characters of inquiry, Rodney and Saxon, had appeared in 1979 following an approach by telephone to the priest to ask if he would bless their union. What the church members describe as hospitality and welcome in the church, they also find in each other. Rodney and Saxon too are described in warm and affectionate tones. They entertained, they invited members of the church to their home, they joined in at all levels of church life and they allowed many members of the church community to see them in a different way from the stereotypical way in which many might have continued to view gay men. Without being provocative or strident, to many in the church community they 'spoke truth to power'. A number of church members testified that because they had known this couple, they had come to an altered perspective of same-gender partnerships.

Healing as sanctuary

The image of hospitality is not unrelated to that of sanctuary. The place of safety is entered depending upon the sense of welcome. The place of safety is encountered because it has marked itself as 'approachable'. Not only does Jesus the healer happen to be in the vicinity of the leper, there is something different about him. His manner makes him approachable and contrasts widely with that of the perceived authorities, who are defined by a negative perception of power. The authorities (who themselves have already rejected the victim) are rejected by the victim in favour of this new encounter. It is precisely this sense of rejection, exclusion and feeling hidden that draws couples to St Luke's. Quite often, at the end of a preliminary preparation meeting, a couple seeking blessing will express relief at the degree of acceptance they have found in the encounter.

> Yes, I was nervous that we were going to be rejected, so I was really pleased when we weren't. *(Paul, Couple 4)*

That sense of safety seems to have encouraged Rodney and Saxon not only to join St Luke's but also to sell their house and move into the geographical parish of the church community that allowed them the sacred space to be themselves. The sense of sanctuary became a seedbed for the kind of values that the church community wanted to develop. Church members of every category saw the value of encouraging faithfulness in partnerships. Several expressed concern with what they perceived to be the damaging consequences of fleeting relationships, promiscuous lifestyles and as one called it, 'the one night stand'. Many of the values sought by St Luke's were styles of living that Saxon and Rodney themselves espoused and wanted to try to live out.

> Saxon Lucas and Rodney Madden are gay, actors, Christians, and have been married to each other for 27 years. Their marriage was blessed by the Reverend Tony Crowe in London at St Luke's church Charlton, in November 1978. When they took their vows they promised to be faithful to one another, to love, cherish and strengthen one another.[4]

This is a view that was borne out in the same article in an interview the couple gave.

> Saxon agrees: 'I think promiscuity in a relationship is dangerous. If you have a good relationship it's worth a damn sight more than a lot of promiscuity.'[5]

However, it was made clear by the members that a place of sanctuary was not merely a manifesto determining other people's personal conduct. One described St Luke's as a place where the boundaries of class and culture were crossed. Another saw it as a place containing wide cultural diversity where the power base seemed to be fairly evenly spread. If Myers' translation of the leper figure in Mark 1 is one that has universal significance (since it raises issues of how we discriminate against people because of their skin and their bodies), then it is pertinent to an image of healing as a place of sanctuary. What happens in the sanctuary of the scriptural encounter is that the excluded one tests the healer's desire to heal. The reaction of Jesus to the leper is one that is usually translated as 'compassionate'. However, some manuscripts recording Mark's gospel use not the word *splagchnistheis* or 'compassionate', but *orge*, which translates as 'anger'. Mark describes in Jesus a deep felt anger that Myers sees rooted in a sense of being put on the spot. Matthew and Luke (who probably used Mark's gospel as a main source when writing their own versions) have dropped all reference to Jesus' feelings. They are not concerned with whether he is angry or compassionate. Others making later manuscripts of Mark may have used the term 'compassionate' because they were embarrassed that Jesus could be angry with a poor leper looking for help! However, Myers suggests that Jesus' anger is not directed at the one excluded but with the system that has forced him to consider either rejecting the excluded (like society and the authorities) or acting in canonical disobedience.

The commitment at St Luke's to being a community of inclusion and reflecting that in a ministry of inclusiveness has been more fully documented in a previous chapter. Body issues (i.e. issues that are concerned with gender and relationship, like the re-marriage of divorcees and the ordination of women) have consistently been met with a willingness to declare the individuals included. On the issue of blessing gay and lesbian couples this declaration has been in marked contrast to the pronouncements of hierarchical Church authorities. Speaking in 1987, the then Chairman of the Board of Social Responsibility, the Bishop of Birmingham, is recorded as saying

> To bless a relationship in church is to bless it in full, in all its aspects — emotional and physical. To bless it is to say God approves of it. The Church cannot approve.[6]

This is something of a redundant argument when we consider some of the things that are blessed. John Shelby Spong makes this point.

> If the conveying of blessing and official approval is the Church's gift to give, then surely that can be given to any relationship of love, fidelity, commitment and trust that issues in life for the two people involved. We have not in the past as a Church withheld blessing from many things. We have blessed fields when crops were planted, houses when newly occupied, pets in honor of St Francis, and even the hounds at a Virginia fox hunt. We have blessed MX missiles called 'Peacemakers' and warships whose sole purpose was to kill and destroy, calling them, in at least one instance, 'Corpus Christi', the body of Christ.[7]

The view of those sharing their reflections was that the strength of an act of blessing lay in the fact that it brought the relationship out of societal shadows and into the light. The effect of this would afford that relationship the opportunity for stability. The prerequisite was that it required a place of safety for it to happen in. The wider benefits of it were seen to be greater societal stability for *all*. It was James, who has been a member of St Luke's since 1943, who recognised that when Rodney and Saxon made their phone call to the rector enquiring after a service of blessing, it was a challenge to the community: 'If you want to, you can declare us included.'

> I think he [the rector] felt Christ would say, 'let them come'. *(James, C1)*

If our reading of Scripture has been consistent, then this elder statesman of St Luke's congregation is probably right.

Healing as liberation

The choice between rejecting the excluded and walking out of step with the hierarchical authorities has been made. St Luke's has chosen to be consistent with the central tenets that mark its story. It is to be a community of inclusion and for that it needs to be not

197

only welcoming and a place of safety, it needs to mark itself as a liberating community, one that empowers the excluded. Such empowerment is healing for both the excluded and the healer. If all are not healed then none are healed. The client system is not a liberating system, it is one in which the excluded remains dependent upon the healer and occupies a solely passive role in the dynamics of the healing context. This is a persistent feature of much of the Church's healing ministry today. Often all that defines it are groups meeting to pray for the sick and services of healing where the 'laying on of hands' is administered. However communities of faith cannot realistically see the life of faith in purely passive terms.

> Faith is not primarily passive waiting on God. It is the active struggle for healing and wholeness amidst the socio-political complexities, ambiguities and conflicts of an industrialised society which makes many people sick and deprives them of real hope in the future.[8]

The leper is empowered not only by being declared clean or by being reincluded in the social fabric of his community, it is also because he is given a job to do. He is to go and 'witness' (speak truth to power) to the authorities that have maintained the power of exclusion over him. He is specifically asked not to spread the word to others, but what happens is the opposite. By notifying the local community the reinstated man effectively calls a press conference and as a result Jesus' movements are restricted, he can no longer move about freely in the countryside. The descriptions by the church members at St Luke's of the changes that occurred within the church community between Rodney and Saxon's service of blessing in 1979 and their twenty-fifth anniversary in 1985 are a mark of the way in which they were evolving as a community of liberating transformation. Some like Mary described how they had really given scant attention to the issues thrown up in the wider Church debate concerning the place of homosexuals within the community of the Church before Saxon and Rodney joined St Luke's. They became close friends. James stated that knowing

Rodney and Saxon helped him to see that this was a matter about real people and real lives.

Others like Millie declared themselves completely altered from their initial stereotypical perception of gay and lesbian couples. The ceremony of blessing was a moment of freeing for the couple, for it allowed them to live openly in a safe community that noted them and affirmed them for who they were together. To that extent it was a service of light that allowed a whole community of people to see a style of relationship in a new way. One might say that the 'body' of same-gender relationships was adopted into the body of Christ in the form of the local church community. Couple and community were ready to witness, to speak truth to power in the form of the body politic. But a problem arose: the body politic was advised of this 'healing' activity through the press.

Part 2 Living with difference
Healing and conflict

In 1979, following the service of blessing for Rodney and Saxon, the Archbishop of Canterbury (Donald Coggan) read about the event in the *Kentish Times*. As senior bishop in England he wrote to the Bishop of Southwark (Mervyn Stockwood) under whose episcopal jurisdiction St Luke's fell. Stockwood in turn wrote to the then rector, Tony Crowe, since the archbishop had expressed concern that the article had alleged that 'gay weddings' took place at St Luke's. Stockwood was clearly under pressure from the archbishop. A gay man himself, he had considerable sympathy for the need to offer pastoral care to homosexual men and lesbian women. He said so in his letter to Crowe.

> It is true we have a duty as priests towards homosexuals, but we also have a duty to those who sincerely take a different point of view.[9]

However, the archbishop's principal concern seems to have been the description of the event as a 'wedding'. Strangely, Bishop Stockwood quotes to Crowe the dictionary definition of marriage as 'the condition of man and woman legally united for purpose of living together and usually procreating lawful offspring'.

What had happened was that the press had broken the news in the only language that it knows – the language of matrimony. The newspaper evidence of the time reveals a certain amount of economy in reporting events as they happened. The *Daily Mirror*'s coverage of the twenty-fifth anniversary celebrations provides an example.

> Protesters stormed the pulpit during a gay 'marriage' ceremony and begged God not to destroy the church after the 'blasphemous service'. The middle-aged homosexual couple Saxon Lucas and Rodney Madden, were half way through the blessing when a man dressed in white robes barged past and pushed the vicar out of the pulpit . . .[10]

None of these actions are verified in the video film that recorded the occasion. However, it set the tone for what happened next. The third section of this healing dynamic (read with a political hermeneutic) reveals itself in the relationship between the healer and the authorities.

There was confusion amongst the hierarchy as to what to do. This was partly caused by their lack of consensus as to where they stood on the issue of same-sex partnerships and partly by the over optimistic desire to present a picture of unity. What happened was that the focus of attention was now removed from the victim and transferred to the perceived healer. The stories generated by the crowds/press required a response, so there was a process of distancing and punitive action. The following extracts from *The Mercury* newspaper of June 1979 amply illustrate this.

> A storm has broken over a vicar's confession that he 'married' a homosexual couple. A bishop admitted this week that he knew nothing of the ceremony. And some church members have called for the sacking of the Rev. Tony Crowe . . . The Bishop of Southwark, the Rt Rev. Mervyn Stockwood, said in a statement that he, 'had no knowledge

of the so called marriages' and strongly disapproved of the term marriage being used.

Mother of two Betty Batchen has called on the bishop to give a full answer. Mrs Batchen said: 'If the local clergy allows Mr Crowe to remain in office without an effort to have such false doctrines removed – may God help us. I regularly attend various churches and since the story appeared, I have met many members who feel Mr Crowe should be sacked.'

The action was also attacked this week by the Rev. Peter Rich, curate at St John's church Stratheden Road. He said, 'While I admire Tony Crowe's courage in conducting the "gay wedding", I also condemn it as being totally opposed to biblical teaching. Homosexual behaviour, like many other weaknesses in human nature can be either overcome, or at least resisted by the power of God.'[11]

If we apply the same political reading for Scripture to this situation then the perceived healer is identified as the rector of the church. He was singled out as the villain of the piece and demonised. The bishop reaffirmed what he (and the archbishop) would uphold as orthodox teaching on marriage. He neither supported nor condemned the rector publicly. Mrs Batchen and Mr Rich stopped short of naming Crowe as a heretic though Batchen described him as a teacher of false doctrine. However, the sentiments are clear. The perceived 'healer' must be silenced. Some called for his removal from office. What I want to suggest is that the criticism aimed at Tony Crowe revealed a misreading of the social and political healing dynamic. While it is abundantly clear that the then rector of St Luke's took the initiative in this pastoral ministry and the church community owes much to his courage in doing so, an error of perception took place. The critics and those who called for his removal were unable to see that Crowe was a single symbol for what the church community he led was implicitly all about. The work that he began was in drawing out the implicit nature of this church's ministry of healing. The single issue of blessing same-gender partnerships was raised to consciousness in the church community but pinpointed and reflected associated issues that have been named in this book. They were issues of justice, discrimination, fidelity and stability. Evidence for this can be seen in the events of 1978 and 1985. In neither service of worship was the rector alone and unsupported, but particularly in 1985 when 100 members of the congregation and families of the two men turned out in support, a shift in congregational consciousness can be seen. Crowe's authority to lead two such celebrations (and the 30 others he went on to conduct) was defined by the experience of the congregation at St Luke's. Living as community with the inclusion of a same-gender couple provided an insight that enabled that community to support the clergy in blessing same-gender couples. The dynamics of the pastoral encounter experienced at St Luke's seem to follow the triangular pattern found in the healing stories of Mark.

My analysis of St Luke's leads me to believe that the signs of healing are located within community life and not simply in the actions of one person belonging to that community. Those actions are not unimportant but they are 'signs' of the implicit nature of the community represented. It is a community that by the translation of its faith ethos into pastoral action provides hospitality, sanctuary and empowerment. It is the community that speaks truth to power. Those seeking punitive action attacked the symbol and not the source.

> Liberation is the fruit of a long process. There are steps that must be taken, and these begin with the praxis of the community itself, a praxis that liberates. The community itself must not be an oppressor but a symbol of freedom of speech, of action, of participation. Otherwise how can you be a sign and instrument for liberation? This new praxis leads to a change in attitudes of the members of the community and not just a change in their actions. These attitudes may lead to persecution.[12]

Healing in the voice of a community

This sense of community as the symbol of healing is one that seems consistent with the way in which the Jerusalem church of Acts saw itself. R. A. Lambourne argues convincingly for a recovered understanding of what it meant for that community to *remember* Jesus.

> So the remembrance of Christ's healing work is not just a remembrance and imitation of his philanthropic act. It is also a repetition of the faith in which he both did it and proclaimed its nature.[13]

He goes on to make the point that it is this corporate act of remembering that is revealed in the incident of healing at the Beautiful Gate (Acts 3). The apostles Peter and John stand for the new community of faith that speaks in the name of Jesus, the remembered one. The power of the faith story that they had lived with Jesus is made present again in the act of remembering. It is this that gives real power to the notion that healing is the purpose of faith communities and that whatever form it takes it is ultimately the activity of inclusion. It is therefore a feature of the healing dynamic that there will always be conflict with those who exercise power/control within the societal system or institution. How that is managed is a mark of that community. Tony Crowe did not lose his job at St Luke's but he was never offered another as a parish priest and it is likely, though not provable, that this state of affairs was not unrelated to the events described here. In a letter to Crowe during his retirement Stockwood spoke of the events surrounding Rodney and Saxon's inclusion into the life of the church community.

> I hope you did not find me too unsympathetic about 'the marriages' which achieved such publicity . . . as you know, I did a lot to help in this matter during my episcopate, but I never appeared in print or joined a campaign.[14]

It would seem that this was true. Stockwood is recorded in the same biography as having conducted a ceremony of blessing for the headmaster of a school and an Anglican priest, which he seems to have done privately and with a degree of informality.[15] There is a sense in which the support of same-gender couples is a *'priestly'* ministry. Care and support have to be administered, and describe this aspect of ministry. But it is clear from the interviews that while there is concern that a degree of pastoral integrity be maintained, this is also a *'prophetic'* ministry. The experience of the congregation at St Luke's was one that never saw them mount a campaign. However, they have made a powerful and challenging prophetic public statement as a community retelling their experiences. It is in marked contrast to the House of Bishops' statement, which seems remote and bolted together. The difficulty for authority figures is that they occupy a different part of the triangle in this systemic analysis. They are caught in their corner trying to maintain two areas of conflicting interest. On the issue of blessing same-gender couples even those who are sympathetic have publicly to declare themselves in line with the agreed statement in order to preserve a picture of unity. In a paper called 'The Church and Homosexuality: Post Lambeth Reflections', delivered to the Affirming Catholicism conference in September 1998, Jeffrey John recounts a conversation with one of the senior bishops in England.

> I tried to remonstrate with one senior diocesan bishop about all this recently. This is a man who passes for a hard liner, but who in private, as he says, doesn't give a damn about what anyone does in bed . . . Nevertheless he voted for the Lambeth Resolution and sticks to the Bishops' Statement like glue . . . When I remarked that this seemed to me a personally dishonest position which would only result in making other people dishonest as well, he became angry and said, 'It's all very well for you banging on about truth and honesty. You're not a bishop. We can't afford the luxury of telling the truth. Our job is to hold the show together.'[16]

Perhaps one reason why St Luke's can make a 'prophetic' statement about the injustice of such a situation is because, as a community with a story to tell, they have tried to handle the emerging differences instead of hiding them. The House of Bishops does not have a community story to tell, it is not a community in that sense. One half seems to terrify the other half simply by being different and it seems to think that by not announcing the differences that this will 'hold the show together'. My analysis of St Luke's is one that leads me to believe that it is not *in spite of* their differences but precisely *because of* their differences that this community remains loyal and does not live with the perennial fear of social and political combustion. I have to say that I think it is precisely because of the experience with gay and lesbian people and with same-gender couples in particular that this is so.

St Luke's, Charlton: Making a world of difference

In an essay entitled 'The Heterosexual Norm', Max Stackhouse[17] argues the case that heterosexual marriage is the norm for the exercise of human sexuality. His appeal is to the creation narratives of Genesis and what he perceives to be the intentions of creation. For him participation in the event of creation is determined by the functional status of the reproductive organs. Following this argument he goes on to assert that homosexual sex is what he calls a terminal sexual behaviour because it does not have the capacity to procreate. What Stackhouse is doing is arguing for relationships of 'other-ness' or difference. The fact that the male body is different from the female body and that together they have the capacity to reproduce is somehow defining of what is the norm. In this case it is heterosexual coupling, best modelled within the institution of marriage.

His arguments are weak on two fronts. Firstly the participation in creation seems to rest upon the ability to procreate. What response might he have for those who either because of age or physical disability cannot have children? What of those who responsibly choose not to have children but whose relationships are nonetheless creative and in other ways fulfilling? Are they any the less participants in the created order? Is sex really the one and only way of being creative?

Secondly Stackhouse has bought into a Barthian view of relation-ship and particularly marriage. Karl Barth's theology of marriage emerges from his understanding of Trinity. God is self-related, three persons in community. What I think this means is that if God is not solitary but communal in being, and creates human beings in the divine image, they cannot be complete as a solitary self. This is not an original thought but Barth argues that in the creation of Adam and Eve it is not a *companion* that Adam needs but a *comple-ment*, someone who is *other* to him and *different* from him. This reflects God's relationship with creation. Because humans are not the same as God, their way of relating to God is as 'other'. For Barth same-gender couples cannot reflect this relationship because they are the same. He maintains that the gay person merely loves in the 'other' a reflection of the self. What Barth has done and Stackhouse seems to have followed is to define likeness and other-ness in terms of the physical body. Certainly as human beings we are embodied and our bodies are important but they do not consti-tute the whole of what it means to be human.

Of all those who took part in this reflection, as has already been seen, only one person defined Rodney and Saxon in terms of their sexual orientation. Instead those who knew them well described them by their individual characteristics. Saxon was more voluble and usually spoke publicly for the couple. Rodney was quiet and reflective but when he spoke it was to say something significant. Saxon could be very dogmatic in his views whereas Rodney would bide his time and adopt a gentle approach to things. These were features that they were well aware of. In the previously quoted article for *New Society*, they are clear about their differences within the partnership.

> Rod is the boss man. What Rod says goes. And when he says 'no' no it is. He is the strength behind me, apart from my Christian faith . . . one of the problems of today is that no-one disciplines themselves in a marriage . . . you have to work at it. You have to learn to compromise, to trust one another and sometimes to hold your tongue.[18]

In all other references to them throughout the interviews they are remembered as a single unit. Rodney and Saxon were gifted, generous, artistic, kind, helpful, entertaining and hospitable. They were pillars of the church. Most descriptions gave a picture of an integrated and well-balanced couple. No one seems remotely bothered that, as a couple, they were created with the same body apparatus. What is consistent about the community at St Luke's is that all relationships formed within the church are met in this way. Much of this is no more than a reflection of the diversity that exists in culture, age and gender. Some of the children who attend are born of mixed race parents; some members of the church are divorced and re-married; some live in relationships that are not defined as marriages; a number live alone either because they are widowed, or never found the partner with whom they could share their lives, or because they were abandoned or simply because they prefer it that way. When the community meets for worship it is revealed as a community of diversity and difference. The members recognise that what they represent is a microcosm of the world as it is. It is no surprise that Rodney and Saxon were met as a couple who were no more peculiar than the rest of the church, parish, national or global community. Differences in lifestyle, background, education, work, family, social habits and countless other things are simply taken as part of what it means to live as a community. One of the teenagers interviewed for this project declared of St Luke's in a conversation outside the interview that he could think of no other gathering in his life where such diversity could assemble and co-exist. I neither claim nor believe that this is unique to the community under scrutiny here. Mark Pryce records his observation of a church community he was invited to address.

> Recently I was participating in a service in church which I found particularly moving . . . though I was a visitor to the church and congregation, nothing I experienced there was strange to me . . . The vicar of this church was a woman, and the priest presiding that day was also a woman. The organist was a woman and all the officers of the church

were women. A man conducted the choir and men read the Scriptures and led the intercessions. The choir was a mixture of people from the local community . . . a good mix . . . this place seemed so full of energy and promise.

I am sure that much of this is due to the skill and devotion of the vicar and the key members who work with her. *But what impressed me was their lack of rivalry.* [Emphasis mine][19]

If the community at St Luke's is one whose members don't feel the need to compete with each other then there will be a healthy respect for difference and perhaps an embracing of it. While it is clear that a greater proportion of those interviewed represented a view that welcomed a ministry of blessing to same-gender couples, they were conscious of others who disagreed and were concerned to see that they were held and respected within the community. However, none of those interviewed felt it best, for the sake of 'holding the show together', that they be dishonest about their differences.

Difference, the stuff that makes us not the same as each other, is identified as a life factor that is critical for the growth and maturity of community life. John Boswell's *The Marriage of Likeness*[20] in which he chronicles a history of same-gender blessings might have been better titled *The Marriage of Difference*. The signs of this reflection exercise are that far from treating difference as something that inevitably leads to irreconcilable disagreement and schism, it is a mark of what it means to be fully human in our relationship with God. Difference is something to be celebrated. Ironically, it is the very openness with which difference is greeted that seems to maintain this community as loyal and united.

Part 3 On 'doing' and 'becoming' the Christian thing

Christopraxis: a way of valuing the corporate experience

A number of church members described themselves as unqualified to do the work of theology, it being perceived as an activity of the professionally educated few. And yet a community of social, cultural, economic and educational diversity at least managed to achieve some theological reflection by discovering a level playing field, and for the community of St Luke's that field and the varying perceptions they had of it was a common experience. There seems to have been a growing movement from 'Christology' to 'Christopraxis'. Christine Marie Smith describes this as

> A movement away from an exclusive and primary conver-
> sation about Jesus of Nazareth and Jesus as the Christ and
> the relationship between these two aspects of our faith, to
> a focus on what it means in our religious lives to embody
> and incarnate redemptive, saving activity.[21]

Christopraxis doesn't replace the work of Christology. Its concern is not principally to discover *the* Christ, but rather more to reflect on images of Christ that emerge from the acting and thinking of communities committed to Christ. What makes it accessible is that it values experience and makes this the starting point for any reflective analysis. It is thus a very inclusive way of seeing and doing the work of theology. For a community that is committed to cultivating an inclusive ethos this method and means of accessing and contributing to theology is a welcome acquisition.

So far this commitment to Christopraxis reveals that the church community has recovered an important story, identified within it consistent themes of pastoral praxis and asked questions of itself about the support and care of same-gender couples. It has dis-covered three models of how it perceives itself as Church. I have argued that the blessing of same-gender unions, when owned by the entire church community, produces dynamics that are almost identical to those found in the healing miracles of Mark if we are prepared to subject them to a systems thinking analysis and a political hermeneutic. In light of this, I have suggested that the current practice at St Luke's be seen as an aspect of the healing ministry. It has allowed a theology of 'difference' or 'otherness' to emerge. What I propose now is to look at what the church community might do in the future to verify its position, develop good practice and confirm its status as an integral agent in the quest for healing and wholeness.

The third way

Gospel texts relating to non-violence have become some of the most misunderstood in the entire Christian Scriptures. As a consequence it has been the fate of Christian tradition to assume that when faced with situations of injustice or oppression, Christians have two options: either they can remain and fight like with like, or they can engage in passive acceptance and argue that it is all part of the divine plan. Walter Wink makes the point that the term 'turn the other cheek' has come to imply a passive, doormat-like quality that has made the Christian way seem cowardly and complicit in the face of injustice.

> 'Resist not evil' seems to break the back of all opposition to evil and counsel submission. 'Going the second mile' has become a platitude meaning no more than 'extend yourself' and appears to encourage collaboration with the oppressor. Jesus' teaching, viewed in this way, is impractical, masochistic and even suicidal – an invitation to bullies and spouse batterers to wipe up the floor with their supine Christian victims.[22]

If the Christian community at St Luke's is to 'speak truth to power' then it has to do so in a way that is a reflection of the Christopraxis already discovered within the community of faith. It was a remarkable feature of the participants' conversations that none of the members nor couples seemed to adopt strident tones or a belligerence in making their views known. Most seemed very gentle and measured in marking their opinions. However there was no sense of passiveness about them. When asked if St Luke's should continue to support same-gender couples with services of blessing – even if it was not a view supported by other churches and the hierarchy – almost all whose views were affirmative stated that affirmation in tones of quiet determination.

> It is uncommon and the wider leadership is divided but I think that it is right to carry on.   *(James, C1)*

> St Luke's should put its neck on the line. It has in the past and it should do now because everybody is entitled to be treated as a child of God.   *(Sally, C2)*

> It is not suitable to have same-sex blessings in every church, but if the congregation accepts that . . . why should they be denied that?   *(Sara, C3)*

> Yes, we can support them, because you can then educate people who are not so sure about homosexuals.   *(Tina, C4)*

> Yes we should. If we don't do something about it, nothing is going to get done.   *(Alex, C5)*

The experience of this community seems to have some common features with the general tenor of Jesus' teaching on resisting injustice. The gospels do not reveal Jesus in the activity of ministry as one who is passive. Wink argues that a possible translation of *'Do not resist evil'* would leave it reading *'Do not react violently against the one who is evil'*. This is quite different to non-resistance of evil, makes more sense of the Scripture and keeps the teaching of Jesus consistent with his pastoral action. Jesus is described as counselling resistance but without violence. The examples that he cites (turning the other cheek, going the extra mile and if you are sued for your shirt, surrender your cloak as well)[23] all follow a pattern. In each the dynamics of power are levelled and the oppressor is shamed. So for example if someone strikes you on the right cheek (an act of insult since it would have to be done with the back of the right hand) then offer the left. The act of insult maintains the power boundary. The superior humiliates the inferior. Offering the left cheek symbolically alters the power relationship. Wink's view is that striking the left cheek can only be done with the fist or the face of the hand – an action made between social equals. An act of non-violence resists one of violence and shames the oppressor.

Where this translates to the context of this enterprise is in the perceived humiliation from a Church that cannot make up its mind as to whether same-gender couples can live openly as couples or even marry – should they wish. It is the perceived humiliation of gay and lesbian candidates for ordination that they have to lie about their partners, be pressed into celibacy, or run the serious risk of not being accepted as candidates for ordination. Examples like the following perception of gay men and lesbian women are all too common. That it was a perception that emerged from a bishops' conference almost seems to make it worse.

> I was meant to be at the Lambeth Conference. I had been invited by the Bishop of Johannesburg to present a paper on the theology of gay relationships to the bishop's section that was dealing with human sexuality. However, I was disinvited the day before, along with others who had originally been invited, because a majority of the bishops had decided that it would give too much credence to gay people to allow them to speak — especially since they hadn't invited paedophiles or bestialists or any other 'equivalent' group.[24]

It was Gandhi who declared that the first principle of non-violent action was that of non-co-operation with everything humiliating. I would contend that faith communities who purport to be communities of healing and value the principles of inclusiveness have no choice other than to adopt this position. Humiliation is debilitating and there is little doubt that many gay and lesbian people feel humiliated by a Church and the places of power in that Church where they are encouraged to remain hidden or speak dishonestly of themselves. Fortunately it has been possible to document the experiences of a few who were treated otherwise and found acceptance within a church community that took them and their relationship seriously. In recognising this, the local church community of St Luke's, Charlton has chosen to continue to support those same-gender couples who approach it and ask for its ministry. The resulting pastoral action is a direct response to a direct pastoral request that reflects the more general need of a social group expressing isolation and rejection.

In doing so, the church community makes no specific claims about or changes to the core doctrines of the Church. However, as the analysis of the material used here has revealed, it is a consequential effect of this pastoral action that the open practice of 'blessing' same-gender couples places the local church in a position that is at variance with other parts of the Church. Most notably this difference is located within certain other local church communities whose pastoral action may be quite different, and the official line of the House of Bishops as laid out in their discussion document *Issues in Human Sexuality*. What highlights these two groups is that, because of their theological positions and the pastoral policies emanating from them, they are often seen by gay and lesbian people (the excluded in this analogy) to be colluding with, if not the source of their humiliation. The effect of the direct pastoral action adopted at St Luke's is to throw light on this dynamic. Those who assume the power that determines which groups are included within the community of the Church and which remain outside are spotlighted and their perspective questioned.

What the local church at St Luke's has done is to decline to co-operate in any action or expressed statement that endorses such a view of gay and lesbian couples. As already seen, this way of looking at pastoral relationships could be applied equally to other pastoral categories (divorcees and women priests have already been cited as examples). Instead St Luke's has chosen to meet the debilitating effects of the humiliation experienced by same-gender couples with its most powerful healing asset, namely the authority to confer blessing. The action of blessing is one that gives public recognition to the couple and often goes a long way to reconciling people who have felt excluded and unwanted. Once again a consequential effect occurs. The action of blessing as a statement of recognition is in conflict with the view of those Church authorities that continue to grant no recognition.

A de-politicised healing ministry, one that takes no account of the power factors, is a passive and probably redundant ministry. Unless we address the questions of what constitutes health and wholeness in the area of human sexuality and determine who decides what illness/brokenness and healing are, we will not be addressing the consequential questions. Those are the questions that decide who is counted in and who is counted out of our faith and wider societal communities and, more pointedly, who has the authority to make those decisions.

CHAPTER 8

Voices Speaking to the Future

images and implications for change

By withholding full recognition of such sexual covenants
the church only, if unintentionally, promotes promiscuity,
for it says in effect, 'Whatever your relationship is, it
is not fit for public Christian affirmation, support, and
celebration'.[1]

James Nelson's words were published in the year that Rodney
Madden and Saxon Lucas arrived at St Luke's, Charlton. The following year the service of blessing and covenanted union began a
new chapter in the local church story. Twenty years later, with the
recovery of that story now documented, the current congregation
has worked to reflect upon it and its subsequent influence on
pastoral praxis.

The conclusions that I am able to draw from this experience
would seem to confirm Nelson's view: stability in human relationships has beneficial consequences for all those engaged in them
and the wider community. This is acknowledged in the bishops'
statement *Issues in Human Sexuality*. However, there is a fundamental inconsistency in any argument that urges stability and
faithfulness in relationships but then declines to endorse that desire
for stability and faithfulness by withholding ritual support.

The urgent need to redress this situation is all the starker in light
of the change emanating from all the major political parties in the
United Kingdom to recognise gay and lesbian partnerships. Even

leading members of the Conservative Party, who have hitherto publicly disapproved of homosexual lifestyles while privately tolerating them (if lived with discretion), have begun to declare open support.[2] Some will see this as a cynical attempt simply to broaden the appeal of a political party. However, what is interesting is the kind of language now in use. Members of Parliament are addressing all forms of discrimination as a 'moral' issue. So if the status of gay and lesbian couples wanting to live in faithful partnerships is deemed to be one discriminated against by law, some MP's perceive the need to address and change that as a moral issue.[3]

> There are people who think that the registration of partner-ships is somehow just further evidence of pandering to a minority, but the reality, as I understand it, the sensible view, is simply that it allows the same rights to be accorded to people of the same sex as heterosexual relationships . . . therefore it follows that it is not an unreasonable proposition if you believe in equality, which I do.[4]

Should legislation arrive by which it becomes possible for gay and lesbian couples, who so wish, to either marry or register their unions in law, there will be serious implications for the Church. The Church of England is a denomination that purports to serve not only its membership, but also the whole nation. If it is unable to recognise a partnership that has become 'lawful', then it leaves a doubtful message. It would seem both to declare itself above the law, sending the message to gay and lesbian couples that though 'lawful', they are still outside of the Church, and also to declare itself selective in its ministry to the nation.

Far from waiting for civil recognition to receive legislation, I would want to suggest that churches should be moving towards providing examples of how these relationships are welcomed and affirmed by the community. The provision of such examples will only come about when local church communities begin to take responsibility for addressing the issues and developing pastoral practices that can adequately respond to them. So, how do we begin to seize back an initiative we should never have lost in the first place?

Discussion and dialogue: a commitment to listening and learning

Perhaps the first thing that might happen is that the 'deep and dispassionate' ten-year study of the question of homosexuality suggested in 1988 by the Lambeth bishops might take place. Certainly the reports of the 1998 conference left even the most neutral observer with the impression that the discussion hardly reflected ten years of preparation. It seems to have been neither deep nor dispassionate. It would be true to say that there has been a good deal of thinking and writing done in recent years in the whole area of theology and sexuality, but little seems to have been driven by the Church. Furthermore, although this valuable work exists as an important resource, much of it remains academic in source and style. The perception of participants in this study was that there was a profound need for information at a basic level. What they have tried to do here is find a way in to a wider study by expressing themselves in an accessible form. For them, that has been through the language of narrative and story in the case of the local church. For the couples it has been through finding a safe space in which to share their experiences. Study is important, but there is limited mileage to discussions about the lives of real people conducted in the abstract. Study alone is not enough. Where real change can occur is at the level of the local encounter. This is where the local community church can make a difference.

The Church with a human face

This is a phrase used by Steve (Couple 4) as a description of what he found as an outsider entering into the life of one local church community. There is something less than human about a Church that has to be so discreet over an aspect of pastoral ministry as to be secretive. It is less than human when candidates for ordination cannot be fully honest about who they are and who is the single most significant-other person in their life. The Church with a human face is one that can cultivate a climate of openness and honesty within itself. Part of this might come about if our pastoral reputation moves from one of tolerance to one of acceptance. Most human beings that are met at the coalface of the Church's ministry are not looking to be tolerated. They seek out the Church because they are in need and look for acceptance. I found a good example of this in a recent encounter.

I attended a football match with a senior clergyman who was visiting the parish. Our local team was well placed for promotion and I had managed to secure some complimentary seats for my colleague and me as guests of the supporter's representative on the club's board of directors. At half-time we were offered hospitality in the bar and introduced to a number of people. One of these was the wife of a director who lived locally. As we were introduced she asked me which was my church. I told her and she continued.

> Oh, I know St Luke's. Dennis and I were married at St Luke's. You see I'm a Catholic and Dennis had been married before, so I knew there would be no point in going to my church. They would never accept us. So I said to Dennis, 'Where can we go? Who will accept us? We have to find someone who will accept us.' Then I said, 'I know, let's go to St Luke's, they'll accept us. They marry gay people there so they're bound to accept us!'

I remember being stunned by her disclosure. For a moment I was quite at a loss in making a response. I was then overwhelmed with admiration and gratitude for her honesty and openness. This was in marked contrast to my own immediate discomfort that someone had announced a ministry at my local church that is usually kept discreet. For me it was a simple act of witness. This is the way we are perceived by some in our local community. I sought her out later and thanked her.

Local church communities need to be open. For many years the pastoral support offered to gay and lesbian couples at St Luke's was chased 'underground'. This was not a happy existence and one that has changed. Openness was a concern for those church members who participated in the reflection process. It led their thinking to a position where they could balance the tension of being honest about what they could support, with the need to avoid the kind of hysterical publicity that had blighted them 20 years ago. Openness was to be reflected in good practice and their recommendations for this were modest, sensible and marked with a concern to see pastoral care offered not only to the couples but also to themselves as a community caring in this way. The details are to be found in 'Appendix A'.

Confronting the 'enemy within'

Confrontation is sometimes perceived solely as the language of the campaigners. Often it has carried the negative reputation afforded it by the angry, if ultimately non-violent tactics of groups like 'Outrage'. However, I want to suggest that it is the responsibility of every Christian to utilise confrontation as a means of challenging possible personal negative perceptions of same-gender relationships. The psychoanalyst Carl Jung used the phrase 'the enemy within'. By it he seems to have meant that humans have a tendency to suppress aspects of the self that they don't really like. These are the things that do not fit the character we choose to present to the world we live in. These are ugly and fearful features of the inner self. They are part of what he calls the human shadow. These emerge in our ability to externalise those features and locate them in other people. It is a root cause of discrimination: in reality, our fear of unacknowledged parts of ourselves. When we offer support for gay and lesbian couples and share services of blessing with them, it is possible to recognise and even integrate some of this shadow side.

Our ministry to gay and lesbian couples at St Luke's is very local. The church community is clear about not being cast as a single-issue church, drawing couples from far and wide. However, this still means that couples may come from other parishes, or churches of other denominations, that would be more locally convenient if their church or parish communities could offer the support being sought. An open policy confronts those churches with the discovery that they too have a ministry to gay men and lesbian women and those who want to be in relationship with each other. Too often this is perceived as a specialist ministry for a minority group of churches. It is not. Openness enables us to see this as a matter for all communities to address and formulate a pastoral response appropriate to that community. A couple of years ago I was invited to speak on our experience at St Luke's at a seminary in Ireland. At the end of the session I was advised by one of the students that gay and lesbian partnerships were not really a problem for the Irish Church. He went on to tell me that if it became a problem they would deal with it by sending it to England. Inner confrontation does not allow this kind of reply. How we care for couples who seek the ministry of the Church is the responsibility of every local church community.

Archbishop Desmond Tutu preached a lot on the unquestionable right to be free. He sees the Gospel of Jesus Christ as subversive of all injustice and evil. In 'The Divine Intention', one of a collection of published sermons, he passionately declares that the right of human liberty is God-intended and concerns itself with broken people. He calls for a transformed society. In the introduction to this collection, Buti Tihagale writes that Tutu's involvement with the struggle aims to bring about a changed moral order built on the foundations of justice.[5] What I am suggesting is that in supporting same-gender partners we are addressing no less an issue of liberty in the wake of injustice and that as such it is appropriate to confront the 'enemy within' in this way.

Strangers and friends

The late Michael Vasey, in his work *Strangers and Friends*,[6] describes a very bleak lot for gay or lesbian Christians. He likens it to that of the crucified Christ, left outside the city. It is a desperate image with which to describe human life and cannot ultimately be a satisfactory one. The cross, despite being the vehicle of redemption, is also the result of human treachery. Christian communities cannot bypass the cross, but neither can they remain there if they are to live as Easter people. This must be reflected in our relationships and more particularly in the way we choose to exercise a ministry of welcome in the Church. Failure to do so is collusion with the treachery that leaves people in crucified isolation. Elsewhere in his book, Vasey suggests some very simple and practical ways of exercising a ministry of welcome to gay and lesbian people. Primarily he suggests trying to understand something of gay and lesbian culture. There is plenty of gay literature available or, better still, get to know someone who is gay or lesbian. Knowledge and friendship are good ways of bridging the gulf of alienation. As we have already seen, this was a factor of major significance in the life of St Luke's. Like many other Christian congregations St Luke's, over the centuries, is likely to have been the spiritual home of some men and women who were gay or lesbian, but who had to live a silent existence. Some may have lived the single life, others as 'companions'. In 1978, that changed when the Rodney and Saxon story became an open story within the church story. Their partnership was blessed through prayer and ritual, and they have been recorded here as being a blessing to many within the church community in which they came to live.

Exorcising the rhetoric of fear

I met Michael Vasey at a conference not long after the publication of *Strangers and Friends*. He looked worn and tired and when I suggested that he must have encountered a lot of flack for writing it, he looked at me and said, 'Oh, yes. The flack is very real.' Not long after, the Lesbian and Gay Christian Movement approached the Provost and Chapter of Southwark Cathedral to ask if they might celebrate their twenty-fifth anniversary at the cathedral. They were welcomed, but that welcome incurred the displeasure of some who at first lobbied to have the decision changed. Prayer vigils were set up, petitions were gathered and one priest wrote a book that he sent to all the clergy in the Diocese of Southwark and to all Members of Parliament in an endeavour to stop the service. The bishop at the time, and others, received vitriolic correspondence. On the night of the service there was a marked contrast between the atmosphere of worship conducted within the cathedral and the shouting of several itinerant preachers who had stationed themselves outside the building to lambaste the congregation upon leaving.

David Atkinson, a noted evangelical thinker and writer, records the response he received from evangelical Christians following the publication of the Osborne Report.

> In 1988 I contributed to the confidential Osborne Report, which offered the House of Bishops a largely descriptive account of the situation in the Church of England at the time. It drew on the experiences of many gay Christians, and presented various options which we thought were available to the bishops. Subsequently, I received what I can only describe as hate-mail from some evangelicals, and I was called upon several times to 'justify' why I had let the side down by putting my name to such a 'compromised' document.[7]

What I have called the 'rhetoric of fear' has played its part in seriously crippling the process of understanding very different points of view, partly brought about by the determination to 'win the argument'. This was the perception of many who either witnessed or participated in the 1998 Lambeth Conference.

> I thought the bishops who worked on the human sexuality resolution at Lambeth came up with a broad, deep, inviting statement that could have been a marvellous document for the whole of Anglicanism. But some folks just couldn't stand to leave it at that: they wanted winners and losers in the Anglican Communion before we went home. I came away from there feeling the tyranny of moving away from in-depth probing and trying to get victory for one side against the other too quickly.[8]

Different Christians from their various traditions might need to persuade themselves that commitment to a process of discovery and discernment, though more difficult, is ultimately more rewarding than manoeuvring in order to 'win the argument'. Thus what we need to do is to become communities of dialogue. This requires giving what we might call contemplative attention to our differences. At St Luke's some attention has been given to this because we participated in an experience and needed to know what it meant to us as a congregation. There were moments of uncertainty and fear, but instead of meeting fear with rhetoric, the community learned in some way to listen to the fear. In 1996 we had a day conference to share dialogue with each other on relationships and how they influence our thinking and being as Church. In 1998 we had an open forum with our near neighbours, a church community very different in tradition and style and view-point on gay and lesbian relationships. In 1999 we decided to discuss in a different way, and to document the experience of retrieving a story and listening to church members and gay and lesbian couples share their experiences. We have moved on a long way from 1979 when the pulpit was occupied and protesters picketed a church service.

Listening to the fear means hearing and acknowledging that saying 'yes' to something does not necessarily mean saying 'no' to something else. Supporting the abolition of Clause 28 does not commit me to an attack on the institution of marriage. The support of same-gender couples does not lessen my commitment to working for the stability of family life. What we must all hear is the fear that some people think that it does, then we can listen to that fear and exorcise it with the clarity of dialogue.

What seems to happen is that when different Christians hear each other take up an opposing point of view their fear is that they will somehow have a valued part of their faith inheritance taken away from them. This perceived 'removal' then poses a threat to their understanding of God, or it may invalidate them and the Christian tradition that has formed them. By listening to the fear beyond that kind of perception it should be possible to reveal it for the lie that it is. What we have discovered in our deliberations locally is that our differences are vital to our for-mation as faith communities, just as difference is vital in the formation of our intimate relationships and friendships as couples. Several contributors in this reflection exercise noted how 'steamed up' other Christians still became when this discussion arises for them. In light of their experience and commitment to reflection they now find it odd to see adult people agitated about something they now see as ordinary. It is time to move on from the name-calling and the rhetoric of fear. We have done all that and it never served us well.

In building communities of dialogue I believe that our experience with gay and lesbian couples can be so integrated as to sound the death knell for an attitude which alienates the couples and pits Christian communities against one another. This is not simply about 'us' and 'them'. It is about all of us.

> How can we live less fearfully and more securely in the grace of God? What is the nature of that loving humanity toward which the Spirit presses us? And what does it mean to be a woman or man in Jesus Christ?[9]

APPENDIX A

Parish Policy and Recommendations for Good Practice

The Way Ahead

All Christian communities need their own definitions of pastoral care and of how it can be shared with others. At the end of this reflection St Luke's was able to draw up recommendations in order to respond effectively to those gay and lesbian couples who ask to have their relationships blessed by the Church. Firstly they noted the following:

1. That it was the desire of the greater proportion of those questioned that St Luke's continue its commitment to supporting same-gender partnerships.
2. That those partnerships be supported as models of faithfulness and stability.
3. That a commitment to seeing such partnerships 'blessed' within the context of an open, welcoming, safe church environment was preferred, and that within such an environment, representatives of the local church community and the clergy would endorse each couple's commitment and empower them to live openly without judgement or prejudice.

Secondly, the conclusions of the reported reflections were presented at a meeting of the PCC on 15 November 1999. After some discussion it was unanimously agreed to receive and endorse the report with a view to adopting its recommendations at the next meeting. This gave all members of the PCC a month to reflect upon the findings before voting.

At a meeting of the PCC on 20 December 1999 further points of clarification were made and a 45-minute discussion ensued. The following memo is taken from item 99/125 of the minutes for that meeting.

It was proposed by Jeffrey Heskins (the author of the research) who declared first that he would not be voting, and seconded by Cyril Young that:

The local church community of St Luke's, Charlton agreed the following principles and adopted them as parish policy at a meeting of the Parochial Church Council on 20 December 1999.
1. That it will undertake to see that all services of covenanted union and blessing between same-gender partners are celebrated openly. That in doing so, it will take care not to attract unnecessary (and adverse) publicity. Measures would include;

(i) Recording such services in the Sunday Parish notice-sheet, as is current practice for opposite-sex couples preparing for marriage.

(ii) Recording such services in the official register of services and in the Parish magazine.

(iii) Praying for the couples at the Sunday Parish Eucharist along with those preparing for marriage.

2. That members of the church liturgy group undertake to draw up a liturgy of covenanted union and blessing for same-gender couples reflecting the theology of commitment uncovered in this research project. They should pay particular attention to the themes of hospitality, sanctuary and empowerment.

3. That agreed (and agreeing) members of the congregation be trained for and included in the preparation of same-gender couples for the services of covenanted union and blessing.

4. That positive effort be made to maintain contact with all couples after preparation and ceremony have taken place to ensure continued support and pastoral care.

This motion was carried, with 9 votes for, 1 vote against and 1 abstention.

' A group of laity representing a cross-section of the congregation, and particularly including representation for ethnic minorities, young people and gay and lesbian members, was convened by one lay member of the congregation. Its task was to create a pastoral liturgy according to the directions of this PCC motion. The results are recorded in Appendix B.

A Pastoral Liturgy for the Blessing of Same-Gender Partnerships in St Luke's Church, Charlton

A Service of Affirmation and Blessing

Music or hymn (optional).

Introduction

Minister: Brothers and sisters, we meet here in the presence of God to celebrate and affirm the commitment of N and N to each other. May they, through the assistance of the Holy Spirit, commit themselves today to each other; promising to live together in love, faithfulness, trust and forgiveness. While they make this solemn covenant we remember that our Saviour Jesus Christ shows us the path of courage and selfless love as we ask God's blessing on their lives. We join in rejoicing with them and offer them support with our love and prayers. Let us hold them in our hearts as we commit their lives to the love and grace of God.

Pause for a moment of silence before the minister continues.

Loving and gracious God, who made us in your image and sent your son Jesus Christ to welcome us home; protect us in love and empower us for service. Through the power of the Holy Spirit may N and N become living signs of his love and may we uphold them in the promises that each will make this day, through Jesus Christ our Lord.

All: Amen.

Minister: Jesus told us to 'Love the Lord your God with all your heart, with all your soul, with all your strength and with all your mind; and love your neighbour as yourself.' For the love that we receive and give let us all thank God, saying together. . . .

All:

EITHER: **Almighty God, source of all being, we thank you for your love, which creates and sustains us. We thank you for your unique and personal gifts to every one of us in our minds, our bodies and our spirits; and for the blessings of companionship and friendship. We pray that we may use your gifts so that we can ever grow into a deeper understanding of love and of your purpose for us, through Jesus Christ our Lord. Amen.**

OR: **Almighty God, source of all being, we thank you for your love, which creates and sustains us. We thank you for the physical and emotional expression of that love; and for the blessings of companionship and friendship. We pray that we may use your gifts so that we can ever grow into a deeper understanding of love and of your purpose for us, through Jesus Christ, our Lord. Amen.**

Music or hymn (optional).

Reading from Scripture
This should be announced as 'A reading from . . .' and ended with 'This is the word of the Lord'.

Questions of Intent
Minister: *N* and *N*, is it your intention to enter into a solemn covenant with each other in love and trust?
Couple: It is.
Minister: Do you offer your lives together for God's blessing?
Couple: We do.
Minister: Will you be to each other a companion in joy and a comfort in times of trouble; and will you give each other opportunity for love to deepen?
Couple: We will, with God's help.

The Promises
Minister (to each partner in turn): Will you, *N*, give yourself to *N*, sharing your love and your life, your wholeness and your brokenness, your success and your failure?

Partner: I will.

Couple: We, N and N, witness before God and this congregation that we have pledged ourselves to each other. We offer you, Lord, our souls and bodies, our thoughts and deeds, our love for each other and our wish to serve you. Take us as we are, and make us all that we should be, through Jesus Christ our Lord.

All: Amen.

Exchange of Rings or Tokens

Minister: God in Heaven, by your blessing let these rings/tokens be to N and N symbols of unending love and faithfulness to remind them of the solemn covenant and promise made today.

All: Amen.

Then each partner in turn presents the ring/token and says:

N, I give you this ring/token as a symbol of my promise, and with all that I am and all that I have, I honour you in the name of God.

Music or hymn (optional).
During this time the couple may sign their wills and/or certificates marking their vows and promises to each other (optional.)

Address

Prayers as appropriate concluding with the Lord's Prayer if there is to be no Eucharist

These might include the following or something similar.

Minister: Loving God, whose son Jesus Christ welcomed strangers and called them his friends, grant to N and N such gifts of grace that they may be bearers of your friendship and their home a place of welcome for all.

All: Amen.

Minister: Jesus, our brother, inspire N and N in their lives together, that they may come to live for one another and serve each other in true humility and kindness. Through their lives may they

welcome each other in times of need and in their hearts may they celebrate together in their times of joy, for your name's sake.
All: Amen.

Minister: Holy Spirit of God, guard and defend N and N in their life together, protect them from evil, strengthen them in adversity until you bring them to the joy of your heavenly kingdom, through Jesus Christ our Lord.
All: Amen.

Minister: Creator God, the source of our being, bless the lives of N and N. May they be faithful and true, generous in the gift of forgiveness, patient and understanding as they grow together, and may they become living witnesses to your restoring love. We ask this in the name of Christ, who heals and sets us free.
All: Amen.

The Lord's Prayer. (*Not when a Eucharist follows.*)

Bidding to the Company
Minister: Will you the chosen witnesses of N and N do all in your power to support and strengthen them in the days ahead?
All: We will.
Minister: God has called us to live with each other in the spirit of love, joy and peace. Let us all share a sign of God's peace. The peace of the Lord be always with you.
All: And also with you.
Minister: Let us offer one another a sign of God's peace.

The company greets N and N and each other.

Music or hymn (optional).

(A Eucharist may follow, the form to be agreed between the presiding priest and the couple.)

The Blessing
Minister: N and N have now given themselves to each other by solemn promises and the making of a covenant. Let us now pray that they may be sustained by God's love.

Spirit of God, you teach us through the example of Jesus that love is the fulfilment of the Law, help *N* and *N* to persevere in love, to grow in mutual understanding, and to deepen their trust in each other; that in wisdom, patience and courage, their life together may be a source of happiness to all with whom they share it; and the blessing of God Almighty, Creator, Redeemer and Sustainer be upon you to guide and protect you and all those you love, today and always.

All: Amen.

Dismissal
Minister: Go in peace to love and serve the Lord.
All: In the name of Christ. Amen.

As the couple and their friends leave, music may be played.

Members of the congregation at St Luke's, Charlton drew up this pastoral liturgy. Some of the prayers in this service have been adapted from *Exploring Lifestyles* published by the Lesbian and Gay Christian Movement. Other material has been drawn from liturgies currently in use at St Luke's.

NOTES

Foreword
1. Nieztsche, *Genealogy of Morals*, Third Essay, section 15.

Chapter 1: **In Search of the Unheard Voices**
1. *Star*, 17 May 1985.
2. *Daily Mail*, 17 May 1985.
3. *Sun*, 17 May 1985.
4. Attributed to the then Prime Minister, Margaret Thatcher, when interviewed on *Woman's Hour*, BBC Radio Four.
5. Michael Doe, *Seeking the Truth in Love. The Church and Homosexuality* (DLT, 2000), 121.

Chapter 2: **The Same Old Voices?**
1. Stephen B. Bevans, *Models of Contextual Theology* (Orbis, 1996), 2.
2. Robert J. Schreiter, *Constructing Local Theologies* (Orbis 1996), 4.
3. Ibid., 4.
4. Stephen B. Bevans, *Models of Contextual Theology*, 13. Bevans cites several sources for a discussion on whether the people are the real theologians.
5. Leonardo Boff, *Church Charism and Power* (SCM, 1985), 131.
6. Stephen Pattison, *Pastoral Care and Liberation Theology* (CUP, 1994), 23.
7. Ibid., 78.
8. Alida Ward Schuchert, *To Give the Kids Religion* (D.Min diss., Princeton Theological Seminary, New Jersey, 2000), 15. Schuchert cites the work of Nancy T. Ammerman, *Golden Rule Christianity*, in defining a bias amongst Generation X churchgoers who value orthopraxis over orthodoxy.
9. Boff, *Church Charism and Power*, 133.
10. *The Church and the Bomb* and *Faith in the City* made radical recommendations and were critical of the governments of the day in the mid-1970s and 1980s respectively. In the case of the latter, one Conservative MP described the findings of the document as Marxist.
11. Jeffrey John, *Permanent, Faithful, Stable* (Affirming Catholicism, 1993), 3.
12. John Shelby Spong and Peter John Lee, 'A Catechesis on Homosexuality', an appendix to *Called to a Full Humanity: Letters to the Lambeth Bishops*, Cristina Sumners (ed.) (LGCM, 1998).

13. Ibid., 38–40.
14. Ibid., 40–45.
15. Ibid., 45.
16. Clare Garner, *Independent*, 6 August 1998.
17. Christopher Morgan, *Sunday Times*, 9 August 1998.
18. Victoria Combe, *Daily Telegraph*, 6 August 1998.
19. Madeleine Bunting, *Guardian*, 6 August 1998.
20. The House of Bishops of the General Synod of the Church of England, *Issues in Human Sexuality* (Church House Publishing, 1991).
21. Ibid., vii.
22. Ibid., vii.
23. Ibid., 41.
24. Jeffrey John, 'The Church and Homosexuality: Post Lambeth Reflections' (Paper presented at the Affirming Catholicism conference, September 1998).
25. Andrew Sullivan, *Virtually Normal* (Picador, 1996).
26. Ibid., 13.
27. Elizabeth Moberly, *Homosexuality: A New Christian Ethic* (James Clark, 1983).
28. Sullivan, *Virtually Normal*, 21.
29. Ibid., 87.
30. Ibid., 97.
31. Gaby Hinsliff, *Observer*, 27 August 2000. Hinsliff reports Conservative Party Vice-Chairman, Stephen Norris, as appealing for a dramatic softening of his party's line allowing homosexual couples to register their partnerships.
32. Sullivan, *Virtually Normal*, 112.
33. Ibid., 184–5.

Chapter 3: Unheard Voices
1. Elisabeth Moltmann, *Women around Jesus* (Pilgrim Press, 1988).
2. James Hopewell, *Congregation: Stories and Structures* (Fortress Press, 1987).
3. Ibid., 47.
4. Leonardo Boff, *Church, Charism and Power* (SCM Press, 1985), 10.
5. John Stott, *Same Sex Partnerships?* (Marshall Pickering, 1998), 31.
6. *Daily Mirror*, 9 June 1979.
7. *Kentish Times*, 7 June 1979.

Chapter 4: Voices in Partnership
1. John Keats, 'Ode on a Grecian Urn'.
2. The Lambeth Conference received the sub-section report on human sexuality on 5 August 1998, at the University of Kent at Canterbury.
3. John 15:15.
4. Mark Pryce, 'On modelling relationships: Jesus, men and friendship', *The Way*, vol. 38, Number 4, October 1998.

5. Mary E. Hunt, *Fierce Tenderness: A Feminist Theology of Friendship* (Crossroad, 1991).
6. Adrian Thatcher, *Liberating Sex* (SPCK, 1993), Chapter 11.
7. Mary E. Hunt, *Fierce Tenderness*, see particularly the section sub-headed 'The Power of Women's Friendships'.
8. Diane Vaughan, *Uncoupling: Turning Points in Intimate Relationships* (Vintage Book, 1990).
9. Ibid., 152.
10. Adrian Thatcher, *Marriage after Modernity* (Sheffield Academic Press, 1999), 294.
11. Tess Ayers and Paul Brown, *The Essential Guide to Lesbian and Gay Weddings* (Alyson Books, 1999).
12. Adrian Thatcher, *Marriage after Modernity*, 302. Here he quotes Johnson from *Daring to Speak Love's Name* (Hamish Hamilton, 1992), 65–6.

Chapter 5: Voices in Harmony

1. Jeffrey John, *Permanent, Faithful, Stable* (Affirming Catholicism, 1993), 20.
2. Ibid.
3. Eric Marcus, *Together Forever* (Anchor, 1998), 151.
4. Frank Griswold, 'Towards Catholicity: Naming and Living the Mystery' in *Living the Mystery*, ed. Jeffrey John (Affirming Catholicism, 1994), 11.
5. Acts 5:34–40, *New Revised Standard Version*.
6. House of Bishops of the Church of England, *Issues in Human Sexuality* (Church House Publishing), 33.
7. Adrian Thatcher, *Liberating Sex* (SPCK, 1993), 145.
8. John Stott, *Same Sex Partnerships?* (Marshall Pickering, 1998).
9. Adrian Thatcher, *Marriage after Modernity* (Sheffield Academic Press, 1999).
10. Ibid., 295.
11. Ibid., 299.
12. Elizabeth Stuart, *Just Good Friends* (Mowbray, 1995), 109, as cited by Thatcher.
13. Genesis 32:22ff.
14. Adrian Thatcher, *Marriage after Modernity*, 300.
15. Ibid. See in particular 245–8.
16. Ibid., 301.
17. Dean Nelson, 'A Gay Marriage', *New Society*, 2 January 1987, 6.
18. Sean Ryan, 'Pulpit stormed as gay couple celebrate their "silver wedding"', *Daily Mail*, 17 May 1985.

Chapter 6: Voices Begging to Differ

1. Quoted in Choon Leon Seow (ed.), *Homosexuality and Christian Community* (Westminster, 1996), 74.
2. See, for example Elizabeth Moberly, *Homosexuality a New Christian Ethic* (James Clark, 1983). Moberly's view is that homosexual feelings are generated because of a poor relationship with the parent of the same

sex. This, she contends, can be rectified by employing a behaviourist therapy in which the client is exposed to positive relational models with members of that same sex.

3. Mike Alsford, *What If? Religious Themes in Science Fiction* (Darton, Longman and Todd, 2000), Chapter 3.
4. Mary McCormick Maaga, *Hearing the Voices of Jonestown* (Syracuse University Press, 1998).
5. Ibid., 23.
6. Mike Alsford, *What If?*, 52.
7. Daniel Migliore introduced this phrase in an open seminar given at Princeton Theological Seminary during a Gay consciousness week in April 1999.
8. Robin Scroggs, *The New Testament and Homosexuality* (Fortress Press, 1983) and Tony Higton's compilation, *Sexuality and the Church* (Hawkwell: Action for Biblical Witness to our Nation, 1987) would provide one example of such a contrast.
9. Mark Taylor, *Remembering Esperanza* (Orbis, 1990), 18.
10. Walter Righter, *A Pilgrim's Way* (Alfred A. Knopf, 1998).
11. Quoted in Michael De La Noy, *A Lonely Life* (Mowbray, 1996), 185.
12. Madeleine Bunting, *The Guardian*, 6 August 1998.

Chapter 7: **Voices Speaking Truth to Power**
1. Paul Ricoeur quoted by Ched Myers in *Binding the Strong Man* (Orbis, 1988), 3.
2. Stephen Pattison, *A Critique of Pastoral Care* (SCM, 1993), 19.
3. Leviticus 12ff.
4. Dean Nelson, 'A Gay Marriage', *New Society*, 2 January 1987, 7.
5. Ibid., 8.
6. Ibid., 8.
7. John Shelby Spong, *Living in Sin?* (Harper Row, 1988), 201.
8. Stephen Pattison, *Alive and Kicking* (SCM, 1989), 102.
9. Michael De La Noy, *A Lonely Life* (Mowbray, 1996), 185.
10. Reporter, 'Wedding of Gays Fury', *Daily Mirror*, 17 May 1985.
11. Reporter, 'Uproar over gay "wedding" service', *The Mercury*, 7 June 1979.
12. Leonardo Boff, *Church Charism and Power* (SCM, 1985), 137.
13. R. A. Lambourne, *Community, Church and Healing* (Arthur James, 1987), 66.
14. De La Noy, *A Lonely Life*, 186.
15. Ibid., 183.
16. Jeffrey John, 'The Church and Homosexuality: Post Lambeth Reflections' (Paper presented at the Affirming Catholicism conference, September 1998).
17. Choon Leon Seow (ed.), *Homosexuality and Christian Community* (Westminster, 1996), 133.
18. Dean Nelson, 'A Gay Marriage', 7–8.

19. Mark Pryce, *Finding a Voice – Men, Women and the Community of the Church* (SCM, 1996), 120.
20. John Boswell, *The Marriage of Likeness* (HarperCollins, 1994).
21. Christine Marie-Smith, *Preaching Justice: Ethnic and Cultural Perspectives* (UCP, 1988), 141.
22. Walter Wink, *The Powers that Be* (Doubleday, 1998), 98.
23. Matthew 5:39–42.
24. Jeffrey John, 'Post Lambeth Reflections', 10

Chapter 8: Voices Speaking to the Future

1. James Nelson, *Embodiment* (Augsburg Press, 1979), 208.
2. Gaby Hinsliff, 'Top Tory backs gay marriage', *The Observer*, 27 August 2000.
3. Ibid., Stephen Norris MP, Vice-Chairman of the Conservative Party, was quoted in this article as saying that he saw 'no moral barrier' to the civil registration of gay partnerships.
4. Ibid., Stephen Norris MP.
5. Buti Tihagale, *Hope and Suffering – Sermons and Speeches by Desmond Mpilo Tutu* (Skotaville, 1983).
6. Michael Vasey, *Strangers and Friends* (Hodder and Stoughton, 1995).
7. David Atkinson, 'Begging to Differ', *Third Way*, December 1995, 18.
8. Pat Ashworth, quoting Bishop William Swing of California, *The Church Times*, 21 July 2000.
9. James Nelson, *Embodiment*, 210.

SELECT BIBLIOGRAPHY

Atkinson, David, 'Begging to Differ', *The Third Way*, December 1995.

Bevans, Stephen B., *Models of Contextual Theology*, Orbis, 1996.

Boff, Leonardo, *Church: Charism and Power*, SCM, 1985.

Bonnington and Fyall, *Homosexuality and the Bible*, Grove, 1996.

Boswell, John, *The Marriage of Likeness*, HarperCollins, 1994.

Brown, Peter, *The Body and Society*, Columbia University Press, 1988.

Campbell, Alistair, *Rediscovering Pastoral Care*, DLT, 1989.

Chopp, Rebecca, *The Power to Speak*, Crossroad, 1989.

De La Noy, Michael, *A Lonely Life*, Mowbray, 1996.

Dulles, Avery, *Models of the Church*, Gill and Macmillan, 1989.

General Synod, *Issues in Human Sexuality*, Church House Publishing, 1993.

Gherkin, Charles, *Prophetic Pastoral Practice*, Abingdon, 1991.

Gottwald and Horsley, *The Bible and Liberation*, SPCK, 1993.

Graham, Elaine, *Transforming Practice*, Mowbray, 1996.

Guggenbhul-Craig, Adolf, *Power in the Helping Professions*, Spring Dallas, 1971.

Hebblethwaite, Margaret, *Base Communities*, Geoffrey Chapman, 1993.

Heyward, Carter, *Our Passion for Justice*, Pilgrim Press, 1988.

Hopewell, James, *Congregation: Stories and Structures*, SCM, 1987.

Hunt, Mary E., 'Significant, So Significant', *The Way*, volume 37, October 1997.

John, Jeffrey, ed., *Living the Mystery*, DLT, 1994.

— *Permanent, Faithful, Stable*, Affirming Catholicism, 1993.

— *The Church and Homosexuality: Post Lambeth Reflections*, unpublished, 1999.

Kane, Margaret, *What Kind of God?*, SCM, 1986.

Kelsey, Morton, *Healing and Christianity*, SCM, 1973.

Lambourne, R. A., *Community, Church and Healing*, Arthur James, 1987.

Loades, Anne, ed., *Feminist Theology: a Reader*, SPCK, 1990.

Lunn, Pam, 'Anatomy and Theology of Marriage: is Gay Marriage an Oxymoron?', *Theology and Sexuality*, volume 17, September 1997.

Lyndon Reynolds, Philip, 'Same Sex Unions, What Boswell Didn't Find', *Christian Century*, January 1995.

MacFague, Sallie, *Metaphorical Theology*, SCM, 1982.

— *Models of God*, Fortress, 1987.

McCormick Maaga, Mary, *Hearing the Voices of Jonestown*, Syracuse University Press, 1998.

Marcus, Eric, *Together Forever*, Anchor, 1998.

Moberly, Elizabeth, *Homosexuality – a New Christian Ethic*, James Clark, 1983.

Moltmann, Elisabeth, *Women around Jesus*, Pilgrim Press, 1988.

Myers, Ched, *Binding the Strong Man*, Orbis, 1988.

Nelson, Dean, 'A Gay Marriage', *New Society*, 2 January 1987.

Nelson, James, *Embodiment*, Augsburg, 1979.

— *The Intimate Connection*, The Westminster Press, 1988.

Pattison, Stephen, *A Critique of Pastoral Care*, SCM, 1993.

— *Alive and Kicking*, SCM, 1989.

— *Liberation Theology and Pastoral Care*, Cambridge University Press, 1994.

Pryce, Mark, *Finding a Voice*, SCM, 1996.

Righter, Walter, *A Pilgrim's Way*, Alfred A. Knopf, 1998.

Russell, Letty, *Inheriting our Mother's Gardens*, Westminster Press, 1988.

Schreiter, Robert, *Constructing Local Theologies*, Orbis, 1996.

Schussler Fiorenza, Elisabeth, *In Memory of Her*, SCM, 1983.

Seow, Choon Leon, ed., *Homosexuality and Christian Community*, Westminster, 1996.

Sheldrake, Philip, *Living between Worlds*, DLT, 1995.

Smith, Christine-Marie, *Preaching Justice*, United Church Press, 1998.

Spong, John Shelby, *Living in Sin?* Harper and Row, 1988.

Stott, John, *Same Sex Partnerships?* Marshall Pickering, 1998.

Stuart, Elizabeth, *Chosen: Gay Catholic Priests Tell Their Story*, Geoffrey Chapman, 1993.

— *Just Good Friends*, Mowbray, 1995.

— *Spitting at Dragons*, Mowbray, 1996.

Sullivan, Andrew, *Virtually Normal*, Picador, 1995.

Taylor, Mark, *Remembering Esperanza*, Orbis, 1990.

Thatcher, Adrian, *Liberating Sex*, SPCK, 1993.

Van de Weyer, Robert, *Celtic Gifts*, Canterbury Press, 1997.

— *Celtic Resurrection*, Fount, 1996.

Vasey, Michael, *Strangers and Friends*, Hodder and Stoughton, 1995.

Ward, Hannah and Jennifer Wild, *Human Rites*, Mowbray, 1995.

Wink, Walter, *The Powers that Be*, Doubleday, 1998.